MINERAL POINT

A HISTORY

MINERAL POINT

A HISTORY

By George Fiedler

Published by
THE STATE HISTORICAL SOCIETY OF WISCONSIN
Madison : 1973

To my wife
AGNES
and our children
MARY AND JOHN

Contents

ILLUSTRATIONS

A selection of photographs illustrating the history of Mineral Point, all drawn from the Iconographic Collection of the State Historical Society, follows page 52.

MINERAL POINT
A HISTORY

Introduction

THE HISTORY of Mineral Point has always been of interest to me. During the last few years I have assembled a collection of books, records, documents and mineral specimens pertaining to the area. I was able to gather a considerable amount of material because the village of Mineral Point is one of the oldest communities in Wisconsin. It occurred to me that others might be interested in the same subject and gradually I evolved the idea of writing a history of Mineral Point. The result is the book presented herewith. In general I have written chronologically. I have quoted extensively from source materials in order to give my readers a vivid glimpse of conditions as they were. I considered carefully whether to give the background of the region or to begin in 1827 when the city was founded. I decided to show the background because of the great antiquity of the lead and zinc deposits in the area.

As to my special interest in writing a history of this particular town, may I say I was born in Mineral Point, my four grandparents and my father and mother lie buried in Mineral Point. My wife and I own a summer home there. On account of this background, I found great pleasure in writing these pages and hope that my readers will enjoy them. If only a few read and enjoy my work, I shall feel that the time spent was well rewarded.

I am indebted to Robert M. Neal of Pendarvis House for his generous cooperation. He has over a period of many years collected an excellent library of books, pamphlets, maps, pictures, letters and numerous original items bearing on the history of Mineral Point. Mr. Neal was kind enough to make his materials available and to offer helpful suggestions.

I wish to express my thanks to the State Historical Society of Wisconsin for permission to use the photographs and the illustrations reproduced in this book. The organization of such a historical society was first suggested and urged by Chauncey C. Britt in *Mineral Point Democrat* of October 22, 1845. In consequence Mineral Point may, perhaps, claim a sympathetic interest from the State Historical Society of Wisconsin.

In particular, I thank Miss Alice Smith, Chief of Research of the State Historical Society of Wisconsin, for reading my manuscript and suggesting many changes. I also thank the Hon. John V. McCormick and Mr. Lewis C. Murtaugh for reading the work and for their constructive corrections.

Finally, I express my thanks to my secretary, Mrs. Gertrude G. Foster, and to my sister, Mrs. Evelyn Fiedler Ketter, for their laborious work in typing the manuscript.

GEORGE FIEDLER

Mineral Point, Wisconsin
and
Winnetka, Illinois
U. S. A. — 1962

Chronology of Areas that Include Present Day Southwestern Wisconsin and Mineral Point

1634   Jean Nicolet, first recorded white man to visit the area that is now Wisconsin.

1654   The area around what is now Green Bay was visited by two French fur traders.

1670   Pere Claude Allouez, S. J., voyaged the Fox River route at least as far as the portage.

1671   Ceremony at Sault Ste Marie at which France announced claims to the Upper Great Lakes Region.

1673   Pere Jacques Marquette, S. J., and Louis Joliet traveled the Fox-Wisconsin route and discovered the upper Mississippi.

1685-   Nicolas Perrot built Fort St. Nicolas at the
1689   mouth of the Wisconsin and claimed the Mississippi Valley for France.

1690   Indians revealed to Nicolas Perrot the existence of lead mines in the Upper Mississippi Valley.

1720-   Francis Renault with a few miners developed
1744   lead mines.

1756-   France and England fought for possession of
1763   colonial empires. Treaty of Paris signed in 1763. France surrendered the vast Northwest areas to England.

1766   Jonathan Carver found quantities of lead in the Sauk village.

1776   Declaration of Independence by the Thirteen American Colonies.

1787   Ordinance of 1787 passed by the Confederation Congress for the government of the Northwest Territory.

1788   Indian Council at Green Bay. Permission to work the lead mines given at Prairie du Chien by the Fox Indians to Julien Dubuque.

1800   This area was part of Indiana Territory.

1805   The Territory of Michigan was organized to include what is now Wisconsin.

1809   This area became part of the Territory of Illinois.

1812   War with England a second time.

1814   England, assisted by Indians, forced the surrender of Fort Shelby at Prairie du Chien.

1816   Fort Howard established at Green Bay and Fort Crawford at Prairie du Chien.

1818   This area again became part of the Territory of Michigan.

1822   First U. S. Government leases to lead miners.

1823   President Monroe appointed James D. Doty United States District Judge for Western Michigan. He held office nine years.

1827   Indian Chief Red Bird surrendered at Fort Winnebago, now Portage.

1827   First permanent settlers at Mineral Point.

1828   Lead ore discovered in the Mineral Point "hill."

1829   Indian title to the lead region in Wisconsin extinguished.

1829   First school at Mineral Point.

1829   Iowa County organized. County seat at Mineral Point, beginning in 1830.

1832   Outbreak of Black Hawk War.

1833   Shot tower completed and operating.

1833   Cornish miners settling at Mineral Point.

1834   Land Office of United States established at Mineral Point.

1834   Methodist congregation built a log chapel.

1835   First visit of Fr. Mazzuchelli to Mineral Point.

1835   County Building for Iowa County in the Territory of Michigan erected at Mineral Point. Built of hewn logs.

1836   First Episcopal services at Mineral Point.

1836   Bank of Mineral Point chartered.

1836   Walker Hotel partially erected.

1836   Territory of Wisconsin organized by act of Congress. Governor Dodge and Secretary John S. Horner took their oaths of office at Mineral Point.

1836　October 25. First territorial legislature of Wisconsin convened near Belmont, about 14 miles Southwest of Mineral Point.

1837　Mineral Point was incorporated as a borough.

1838　Odd Fellows Hall (Iowa No. 1) erected at Mineral Point. It was the first chapter west of the Allegheny Mountains.

1841　The Bank of Mineral Point failed.

1841　Mineral Point Lodge No. 1 Free and Accepted Masons received its dispensation.

1842　First Catholic Church erected at Mineral Point. St. Paul's Parish.

1842　Fourth territorial legislative assembly. Moses M. Strong of Mineral Point elected president of the council.

1842　William Caffee legally hanged on a scaffold in the lower part of Mineral Point.

1842　Second County Building erected with native limestone.

1844　Date of village charter to Mineral Point.

1845　St. Paul's stone church completed; blessed December 7, 1845.

1847　The *Mineral Point Tribune* began publication.

1847　Mineral Point Academy gave instruction in Greek, Latin, French, English and mathematics.

1847　Population of Mineral Point was 2,946.

1848　Wisconsin became a state.

1848 Primitive Methodist Church organized at Mineral Point, now the Congregational Church.

1849 Exodus from the Mineral Point lead mines to the California gold mines.

1852 Mineral Point Railroad Company was chartered.

1853 Fifty new buildings erected in Mineral Point in one year.

1854 William Rudolph Smith of Mineral Point published Vol. I and Vol. III of the *History of Wisconsin*.

1857 Railroad completed into Mineral Point.

1857 Mineral Point received its charter as a city.

1860 Population of Mineral Point was 2,389.

1861 Shot tower closed.

1861 The *Mineral Point Tribune* carried the story of the bombardment of Ft. Sumter and the beginning of the Civil War.

1861 County seat moved from Mineral Point to Dodgeville.

1861 Mineral Point Railroad went into receivership.

1862 Supply of lead ore in Mineral Point area diminishing.

1865 The *Mineral Point Tribune* carried the news of the end of the Civil War.

1868 Telegraph line completed to Mineral Point.

1870 Population of Mineral Point was 3,275.

1870 St. Mary's parish erected frame church and frame rectory.

1874 Primitive Methodist Church dedicated.

1878 Tornado swept over northern edge of Mineral Point.

1880 Population of Mineral Point was 2,915.

1882 Mineral Point Zinc Company founded with capital of $35,000.

1883 David B. Jones, William A. Jones and Thomas D. Jones bought Mineral Point Zinc Company and increased its capital to $400,000.

1885 Moses M. Strong of Mineral Point published *History of The Territory of Wisconsin.*

1890 Population of Mineral Point was 2,694.

1890 Floods struck the lower area of Mineral Point. Four miles of railroad track severely damaged.

1891 Electric lights in Mineral Point.

1893 Financial panic in U. S. A.

1897 Fire swept through several buildings on High Street. Damage about $35,000.

1897 Mineral Point Zinc Company sold to New Jersey Zinc Corporation.

1899 Mineral Point and Northern Railway Company incorporated. Owned by Charles W. McIlhon, William A. Amberg and Donald Morrill.

1900 Population of Mineral Point was 2,991.

1902   St. Mary's parish built its second church.

1905   High School built of hand cut limestone blocks. Dedicated. Address by E. C. Fiedler.

1908   Thirty-three lead and zinc mines operating in Mineral Point area.

1909   The First National Bank of Mineral Point closed its doors.

1910   Population of Mineral Point was 2,925.

1911   Locomotive of Mineral Point and Northern Railroad fell through bridge west of Highland Junction.

1913   Court House at Mineral Point demolished. Erection of present Municipal building.

1917   United States entered World War I.

1918   Armistice ended World War I.

1920   Population of Mineral Point was 2,569.

1925   High School (present building) completed.

1927   Mineral Point celebrated its centennial.

1929   The great economic depression began.

1932   The Consolidated Bank of Mineral Point closed its doors.

1938   The *Mineral Point Tribune* and The *Iowa County Democrat* were consolidated.

1939   Hope Lutheran parish founded at Mineral Point.

1940   Population of Mineral Point was 2,275.

1941   United States entered World War II.

1945   Hope Lutheran Church dedicated.

1945   End of World War II.

1950   Population of Mineral Point was 2,284.

1959   High School enlarged, improved.

1960   Population of Mineral Point was 2,384.

1962   This history completed.

I.

Prehistoric Background

The Deposits of Lead and Zinc

THE FORMATION in the rocks of lead and zinc deposits extends back immense periods and eras in time. The Ordovician period of the Paleozoic era began approximately 480,000,000 years ago, and during that period the deposits of lead and zinc, and some copper, were formed in the area which is the subject of this book. The geological evolution continued with one great period of time followed by another until enormous ice sheets crept from the polar regions southward and vast regions were covered by glaciers, about a mile thick. The great weight of the glaciers pushed rocks and boulders and gravel ahead. There was, however, one unique area of about 15,000 square miles that probably escaped the earlier glaciers, certainly the last glacier. It is sometimes called the driftless area, because the last glacier never drifted over it. This pocket or enclave of land is one of the most puzzling prehistoric facts. A theory has been advanced that in prehistoric times both Lake Superior and Lake Michigan covered much larger areas than today; that as the glaciers moved south they followed the beds of the lakes and went around the region that is now

Southwestern Wisconsin; that the last glacier missed, and thus left, a small area in its ancient condition, rich in lead and zinc ores. Thus Southwestern Wisconsin remained a small island of land in an immense sea of ice.[1]

The difference between the glaciated and unglaciated areas can be seen sharply if one travels from the east to the west on present Highway 11. The Sugar River forms the dividing line. East of the Sugar River the terrain was flattened by the last glacier as it drifted over. There the glacier, as it melted, deposited rounded granite boulders and rounded gravel on top of the leveled earth. The debris had been picked up hundreds of miles to the north and had been carried and ground in the glacier as it flowed and drifted south. The granite boulders and gravel dropped on the surface are from an entirely different rock formation than the sedimentary formations deep below. So it is that east of the Sugar River one sees today the foundations for houses and barns built of red, grey and black granite boulders, rounded and weathered.

West of the Sugar River there are no such boulders. Not one. The terrain is not level but hilly. The rock formations are sedimentary, deposited ages ago, long before the glaciers, and these fixed formations are of various kinds of limestone and sandstone. West of the Sugar River foundations for houses and barns were built of quarried limestone or quarried sandstone.

It is certain that the small driftless area is very old, certainly the oldest thing on the face of the earth in the Middlewestern United States.

The topography of this particular part of the driftless area is simplicity itself. There is a high ridge, a watershed, identified successively as the Old Ridge Trail, The Military Road, and now U. S. Highway 18. It runs from the high bluffs overlooking the confluence of the Mississippi River and the Wisconsin River, due east for about 85 miles. Mineral Point lies eight miles south of that ridge. Numerous delightful hills, ridges, valleys and streams intersect at varying angles; the trend of all of them is south towards the Pecatonica River, which flows into the Rock River, which flows into the Mississippi, which finally flows into the Gulf and the open sea. The average annual rainfall is 31 inches and the snowfall is 45 inches.

Mineral Point lies at an altitude of 1,135 feet above the sea. The highest elevation in the area is West Blue Mound, half again as high with an elevation of 1,716 feet above sea level; and towards the southwest are three more mounds, Belmont Mound, Platteville Mound and Sinsinawa Mound. The four mounds stand like sentinels capped with a layer of hard limestone, about 100 feet thick. Geologists say that this hard limestone once covered the whole area but was eroded away through the ages, excepting the accidently preserved four mounds. A cross section of any of the mounds and the rock formations beneath would show alternate layers of limestone and sandstone, including the Galena-Trenton limestone, which is the formation in which the lead miners were most interested.[2]

This ancient unglaciated area contained lead, one of the heaviest, softest and most useful metals. Lead is bluish-gray, easily melted, very malleable. For ages, lead has been used to make plummets to gauge the depth of the sea, to make paints in ancient Egypt, to make lead pipes in Roman palaces and baths, to make medicines, to cover entire roofs, to make ammunition and other materials of war, to make solder, to make pewter, to make printing type, and in more modern times has been put to use in the electrical industry.

The area also contained zinc, a bluish-white metal used through the ages in medicines, in paints, and in coating and treating other metals. Several theories have been advanced to explain how the deposits of lead and zinc were created. Some scientists say that the minerals were formed hydrothermally during the Ordovician Period by hot percolating waters which contained the dissolved metals in solution. Other scientists adhere to a theory of lateral secretion of cold waters.

The most ancient prehistoric dwellers in this area were the Indian mound builders, so called because they left behind them artificial elevations of mounds of earth. These elevations sometimes rise as high as six feet. Some are geometrical figures, such as the square and circle; others, called animal mounds, resemble animals, reptiles, birds and man; all of them are effigy mounds in the totemic system. Some of the mounds were used for burial purposes, but the greater number of them were found to be empty of bones. Many relics of the mound builders have been found, including stone axes, copper axes, and other artifacts. It was formerly believed that many such relics showed an art, skill and intelligence beyond the Indians who were here when the area was discovered by the white man, but more modern anthropologists believe the mound builders were not a separate race but American Indians.[3]

Apparently the Indians did not build a village in the immediate vicinity of present-day Mineral Point; the Indians merely passed through this locality when on the hunt. The old Jerusalem Spring (as subsequently named) was well known in the early days for its pure, potable, and plentiful drinking water. Iowa County got its name from the early "Ioway" Indians, who possessed immense areas of wilderness. They were followed successively by the Winnebagoes, Sacs, and Foxes. Years later the white settlers, who broke the land and exposed the soil, would after each cultivation and rainfall, find an occasional arrowhead, less frequently the stone of a war club, and very rarely a copper pick axe. When the author of this history was a boy at Mineral Point, many local families had at least a small collection of Indian arrowheads. Unfortunately many of those collections have, through lack of interest, been lost or discarded.

Lead was known to the prehistoric Indians but was not prized; they had little use for lead. Considering the abundance of lead ore and the ease with which it could have been dug from surface outcroppings, very few lead artifacts have been found. A few turtle effigies and other items comprise all the prehistoric lead items found in what is now Wisconsin, and the origin of those few objects is doubtful. Although it is an almost incredible fact, there is absolutely no evidence that the aboriginal inhabitants in what is now Southwestern Wisconsin made any considerable use of lead prior to the appearance of the French explorers and traders.[4]

The next chapter will deal directly with early recorded history of this region and will begin with a discussion of the French.

NOTES

[1] Wright, G. Frederick, *Man and the Glacial Period* (New York: D. Appleton and Company, 1889), pp. 99-103 *passim*.

[2] *History of Iowa County, Wisconsin* (Chicago, 1881), p. 111.

[3] Raney, William Francis, *Wisconsin, A Story of Progress* (New York, 1940, Prentice-Hall), p. 8.

[4] Kellogg, Louise P., *The French Regime in Wisconsin and The Northwest* (State Historical Society of Wisconsin, Madison, 1925), p. 359.

II.

Discovery. The French, The English, The United States

RECORDED history began about six thousand years ago and many civilizations had seen their rise and fall before the white man discovered this part of the world. If one will visualize recorded history as a straight line of six thousand feet, the written records about this area are almost at the end.

In the days of the explorers two great mother countries had importance for this region, France and England and in that order. Spain should be mentioned if only to be put aside. Spain made its discoveries in the southeast of what is now the United States in 1492, made a permanent settlement there in 1493, entered into the Treaty of Tordesillas in 1494, dividing the new world with Portugal. Spain laid legal claims to enormous lands, including even what is now Wisconsin, but it is probable that not a single Spanish explorer ever ascended the great river as far as the upper Mississippi lead region. Nevertheless the shadowy legal claims of Spain continued until they lapsed or were abandoned or ceded.

France explored and settled the wilderness in this region. French Jesuit missionaries and French fur traders moved through the St. Lawrence River and the Great Lakes in a generally southwesterly direction.

One can imagine the long arm of Spain from the southeast and the longer arm of France from the northeast almost meeting in the present day Middle West. Still it was the Kingdom of France and the French Jesuit missionaries and the French fur traders who were first whites to come to this region.

At this point it should be made clear that in the days of inland exploration it was much safer and easier to travel by water than over unknown land inhabited by savages. At the time of the explorations by the French one could travel through the St. Lawrence River, thence through the Great Lakes passing Mackinac Island, thence to what is now Green Bay. There a river (the Fox) leads and flows northeast and empties into Green Bay. By following that river southwesterly and upstream one comes to a point where, only one and one-half miles to the west, there is another river (the Wisconsin) which flows in an opposite direction. These two rivers flow in opposite directions but constitute a trough of water diagonally across Wisconsin for 300 miles from the northeast to the southwest. The very short distance between the two rivers was swampy lowland, a portage, easy to cross with canoes and baggage. Ordinarily the Fox was three feet lower than the Wisconsin; however, during the spring thaws and freshets, the waters of the two rivers would actually unite and canoes could be floated across. Even in dry weather, during low water, when canoes and baggage had to be carried, the portage was an easy one. By canoe, the trip across what is now

Wisconsin required about seven days, either way. That was the route followed by the French missionaries and explorers and fur traders from the northeast to southwestern Wisconsin. At one end of the historic waterway was Green Bay; at the other end was Prairie du Chien. Both towns began as French missions and fur trading posts. Later both towns and the connecting waterway were important in the lead trade.

Jean Nicolet, in 1634, was the first white man to reach what is now Wisconsin. Thirty-six years later in 1670, Pere Claude Allouez, S. J., a French missionary, traveled from the northeast towards the southwest and journeyed the route of the Fox River at least as far as the portage.

Only three years later in 1673, Pere Jacques Marquette, S. J., another missionary, and Louis Joliet traveled the same route, crossed the portage and went all the way to discover the confluence of the Wisconsin and the Mississippi. Thus a French Jesuit missionary and a French trader came within thirty miles of the Mineral Point area. Mineral Point's own historian, William R. Smith, wrote about Father Marquette and his companions:

". . . Marquette and his companions addressed themselves in prayer to the Holy Virgin, which devotion, he meekly says, they practiced daily, placing under her protection their persons and the success of their voyage. After having encouraged each other, they stepped into their canoes and boldly embarked on the bosom of the Mescousin, since known as the Ouisconsin; but when or in what manner the name was altered is not accurately ascertained. . . . This river is described as very wide, with sandy bottoms, causing many banks, and rendering the navigation very difficult; full of vine-covered isles, and bordered with fine lands, comprising woods, prairies and rising grounds. The adventurers found roebucks and buffalo in abundant numbers, and perceived appearances of iron-mines.

"After a navigation of forty leagues on this river, on the 17th of June, 1673, 'with a joy,' says Marquette, 'which I cannot express, we happily entered the Mississippi, in the latitude of forty-two degrees and a half.'"

"It is somewhat remarkable that, during the whole course from the portage to the mouth of the Wisconsin, Marquette neither saw an Indian village, nor met with a native Indian . . ."[1]

In the light of present knowledge it now seems probable that Marquette did not see evidence of iron or lead mines.

A few years later in 1690, Nicolas Perrot definitely discovered the lead region. In that year, a friendly Indian chief gave Perrot some lead ore saying that it came from a rich lead mine on the banks of a stream which empties into the Mississippi. Perrot pretended to be uninterested but was secretly pleased. He followed his Indian guide and found the mine, somewhat below the mouth of the Wisconsin, the exact site being lost in time. Perrot taught Indian squaws to break the rocks by heating them and pouring on cold water, thus separating the lead ore. He also taught the squaws to melt the ore in crude and primitive smelters which were simply piles of logs with the ore heaped in the center. The molten lead ran into a place scraped in the earth below, thereby forming flat pieces known as plates, each weighing from thirty to seventy pounds. From Perrot's discovery in 1690 and throughout the French regime, both Indians and the French worked the lead mines. The product of the lead mines supplemented the fur trade.[2] When later the whites entered the lead region in large numbers some Indian shafts or diggings still contained crude ladders which had been made by felling a tree and cutting the limbs back to serve as rungs.

In the next century, in 1720, Philippe Francois Renault came from Paris to the lead region and opened several good mines. In 1744, he sold his holdings and returned to France.[3]

Perrot and Renault saw a landscape substantially the same as it is now. They saw numerous hills, valleys, small streams, eroded bluffs and old weathered rocks. A few small prairies covered with tall grasses spotted the area. In this ancient, interesting and beautiful region, small groves of oak and maple were scattered about but there were no great forests.

The 1600's and 1700's were times when the history of this region was exclusively French and written in French. Many Wisconsin lakes, rivers, and settlements bear French names, attesting to the importance of all things French in these early days. The rule of France ended when France was defeated by England in the wars for the possession of colonial empire, and in the subsequent Peace of Paris in 1763, France ceded to England the vast regions east of the Mississippi, including what is now Wisconsin. It was the end of the French regime, the end of a romantic era. It had lasted more than a hundred years. During that time the few and scattered settlers were French, or French Canadian or half-breeds of mixed French and Indian blood.

The victorious English began to rule these sparsely settled lands in 1763. The English found only a few families of Anglo-Saxon heritage and these lived at Green Bay. A few years later in 1766 and 1767 a New Englander named Jonathan Carver made a voyage which resulted in the first description of this region in the English language. Carver traveled the Fox-Wisconsin water route. He visited the Indian village of the Saukies, the present-day Sauk City, and found pieces of lead lying about. It was float mineral, taken from surface outcroppings. Apparently the Indians had little use for it. The English rule of this region was very brief, because in 1776 came the Declaration of Independence and a few years later the defeat of England. By the peace treaty of 1783, England ceded the northwest areas to the United States and the Great Lakes were fixed as the permanent international boundary between the British Canadian possessions and the United States possessions.[4]

The Congress of the Confederation adopted the "Ordinance of 1787" for the government of the Northwest Territory. The great act provided that in time three to five new states should be formed out of the territory, that education should be encouraged, that religious and political liberty should prevail, and that slavery should forever be prohibited. Thereby the vast Northwest Territory, most of it still owned by the Indians, came under the paper rule of the United States. The region was almost empty. According to one estimate made in 1796, fifteen thousand white inhabitants lived in the enormous space between Pennsylvania on the east and the Mississippi on the west, and from the Great Lakes down to the Ohio River.[5]

The Congress of the United States proceeded to organize the Northwest area into territories. In 1800,

22

the area that now embraces Mineral Point was technically part of the Indiana Territory. In a note appended to the census for the Territory of Indiana appears the following: "On the 1st of August, 1800, Prairie du Chien, on the Mississippi, had 65, and Green Bay 50 inhabitants."[6] In 1805 this region was part of the Michigan Territory. In 1809, it was part of the Illinois Territory. In 1818, it was again annexed to Michigan.

During the long French regime and the relatively short British rule and the few years of the post-colonial period, the essential character of the region changed little. The definitive change occurred when the English speaking southerners and Yankees quite suddenly occupied the area. That change marked the beginning of another chapter in history.

NOTES

[1] Smith, William Rudolph, of Mineral Point, *History of Wisconsin*, 1854, Vol. I, p. 36.

[2] Kellogg, Louise P., *The French Regime in Wisconsin and The Northwest*, (State Historical Society of Wisconsin, Madison, 1925), pp. 359, 360.

[3] *Ibid.*, p. 361.

[4] Usher, *Wisconsin*, Vol. I, p. 9.

[5] *Ibid.*

[6] *History of Iowa County, Wisconsin* (Chicago, 1881) p. 258.

III.

The Founding of Mineral Point in Michigan Territory in 1827

The Lead Diggings

THE LEAD region, when first settled by whites, was pock-marked at many places by the old Indian diggings. Relics of a primitive Indian furnace were found at a point which lies immediately northeast of present day Mineral Point.[1]

In the early 1800's lead miners from the Missouri and Galena mines, most of them southerners or Yankees, moved progressively north from Illinois across the line into this area, then in Michigan Territory, but owned by the Indians. It has been reported that tombstones have been found at what is now Mineral Point, showing deaths at that place in 1808, 1812 and 1820.[2] However, no supporting written records have been found and the evidence of any permanent settlement at this point by whites during those early years must be considered apocryphal. There is a scintilla of evidence that in 1820 white people opened lead mines at what is now Mineral Point.[3]

The prospectors ignored the rights of the Indians and found and opened lead mines on lands owned by

24

the Winnebago. This caused an Indian uprising, sometimes called the "Winnebago fuss." However Chief Red Bird surrendered at the fort at the portage on September 3, 1827, and immediately afterwards the miners became much bolder and entered the lead region in considerable numbers, again ignoring the ownership by the Indians, and this influx brought events to the founding of the town of Mineral Point.

In 1827, Elder William Roberts, who was a Baptist minister, Solomon Francis, Christopher Law, and perhaps a few others began prospecting in this immediate vicinity, built two cabins, and became the first permanent white settlers. A later settler wrote:

"When we arrived there, we found two cabins already built and occupied. The first was erected in the summer of 1827 by a Calvinistic Baptist minister named William Roberts, and an associate, one Solomon Francis. The other cabin or hut was owned by a German by the name of Christopher Law . . . ." [4]

It is certain that those three white settlers began living here in 1827; and the recorded and corroborated history of the first permanent settlement dates from that year. The settlers erected two cabins near the historic "Jerusalem Spring." Elder Roberts was a preacher and an ardent leader of stirring Christian hymns, especially "Jerusalem My Happy Home" which he led in singing over and over again.[5] The gushing spring would become known as the Jerusalem Spring and the block around it as Jerusalem Park.

In 1827 Henry Dodge of the Missouri lead mines came north with his wife and nine children and his slaves to the upper Mississippi mines and settled a few miles north of Mineral Point. Within a year he and his slaves had erected a stockade and opened mines; they raised a ton of ore a day and operated several log smelters. The story of Henry Dodge and his splendid record of achievement will recur frequently in the subsequent pages of this book.

In the early summer of 1828, John Hood and his wife arrived here, built a rude hut and stayed. Also in 1828, a few miners arrived, began prospecting, digging here and there, haphazardly "dowsing."[6] Dowsing means to search for minerals with the use of a divining rod. Dowsing is a Cornish word derived from the Low German or English "deusing rod." At Mineral Point the miners would cut a forked stick from a small hazel or willow tree, hold each branch in one hand and walk about until the stick turned in their hands and pointed down. As a boy this writer saw much "dowsing" and always marvelled at it.

As to the appearance of the settlement, according to Edward Bouchard:

"In July, 1828, I camped . . . one night while on my way to Sugar River, where I afterwards took up my abode. At that time, I saw no one at the Point, except three men who were erecting a log cabin. I remember only the names of two of them, Messrs. Blackstone and McMurrish. I am quite certain that, for so far as I am aware, mineral had not then been discovered here, and consequently nearly all of the miners, like myself, were inclined to go where they were well assured lead had been found, rather than to spend their time in prospecting.

But, after all, the most of the people were coming and going from place to place constantly, trying to find better diggins or locations . . ."[7]

Late in the summer of 1828 Nathaniel Morris and a man named Tucker and another named Warfield, struck lead ore in outcroppings or shallow diggings in the hill directly east of the first settlement.[8] The ore was found in chunks of almost pure lead. The chunks, when broken open, usually consisted of cubes of the mineral and were brighter than the most polished silver. This lead ore was sometimes called galena, more often simply mineral. The news of the strike spread quickly. Miners, merchants, speculators and adventurers were sure to follow.

In the fall of 1828, some merchandise was brought to the new settlement by a man named Erastus Wright, who erected a log house as the first general store. Also in 1828 a physician, a Dr. Mannegan, arrived.[9]

In 1829 there was an influx of miners and other settlers, all of them squatters on land still owned by the Indians. They erected several primitive cabins around Jerusalem Spring. The miners also built a few crude huts on both sides of what would soon become known as Shake Rag Street. Thus there were two primitive settlements separated by a distance of half a mile. The village grew haphazardly. In 1829, miners discovered lead ore in many shallow diggings in the hill. There is a small stream on the near side of the hill, a slightly larger one on the far side. The two streams join about one hundred and fifty yards south of the bluff or point at the southern end of the hill. The miners came here, worked the mines in the hill, and by common consent called their settlement Mineral Point. William R. Smith, an early settler, wrote a letter to his brother and explained the origin of the name, thus:

"The town takes its name from a hill or extension of the upland prairie lying east of the ravine, through which flows a branch of the Petketonica. (sic) On this hill the first lead diggings were opened and they still continue to be worked to great advantage. The hill divides two small branches of the Petketonica and terminates abruptly south of the town where the streams unite, hence the name of Mineral Point."

The very name of the place carried with it the thought that the settlement was a mining camp. It also had a nickname, Shake-Rag Under the Hill. Miners occupied the cabins at the foot of the hill and at noon the women folk would shake a rag and signal to their men at work in the diggings on the opposite hill that it was time to come home for dinner. The name "Shake Rag" was commonly used in the early days, then dropped, more recently revived.

One of the early settlers was Daniel M. Parkinson, who was born in Tennessee, moved to southern Illinois, then to northern Illinois, next to New Diggings, and shortly afterwards to Mineral Point. According to his own statement:

"Removing, in 1829, to Mineral Point, I opened the first tavern ever kept in the place. Mineral Point was then the great centre of attraction to all miners: some of the largest leads were struck and extensively worked, and quite a number of mining and smelting establishments erected there and in that vicinity. . . . The town grew up with great rapidity, and everything wore the most pleasing and encouraging aspect. The anniversary of American Independence was this year celebrated at Mineral Point with great pomp and ceremony. . . . There were at least a thousand persons in attendance; the orations and ceremonies were as fine, as well timed, and all as happily adapted to the occasion, as any I have since witnessed in this country." [10]

Later in 1829 the Legislative Council of the Territory of Michigan, sitting at Detroit, created Iowa County, comprising all of what is now southwestern

Wisconsin; and Mineral Point became the county seat of the enormous new county. Law became a reality. The important story of Mineral Point as a county seat and the efforts to keep the county seat will be told in a later chapter.

Other events are recorded in 1829. Lovey Roberts, a daughter of Elder Roberts married Joshua Brown.[11] On November 29, 1829, a son was born to John Hood and his wife in their sod hut. The infant, named John Theophilus Lawson Hood, was the first white child born in Mineral Point. Elder Roberts, the Baptist preacher, erected a log building west of the Jerusalem Spring to be used for religious services and in which a Protestant school might be kept. This primitive structure was also used as a general meeting place.

In 1829, R. W. Chandler of Galena published an extraordinarily interesting map entitled "Map of the United States Lead Mines on the Upper Mississippi River."[12] It showed graphically:

That Northwestern Illinois and Southwestern Michigan Territory formed a lead region, dotted with miners' camps and claims.

That the United States owned the land and the lead mines in fee simple; that commissioners had been appointed to extinguish the Indian title.

That the mines were worked by private individuals who paid the Government a tenth of all lead manufactured.

That a lot six hundred feet square was allowed to every two miners and an additional lot for every two hands employed; the occupants had the exclusive benefit of their discoveries but could sell lead ore only to a licensed bonded smelter who had to pay a tenth of all lead smelted to the United States Government.

That the lead miners were entitled to the free use of government timber for building and for fuel.

That the same person could be miner, lessee, smelter or all together.

That farming was permitted free of rent, wherever it could be done without interfering with the timber needed for mining purposes.

That "Mining is as simple a process as the common method of digging wells."

That the amount of lead manufactured was:

In 1825	439,473 pounds
In 1826	1,560,536 pounds
In 1827	6,824,389 pounds
In 1828	12,957,100 pounds

That the estimated population of the entire lead region was:

In 1825	200
In 1826	1,000
In 1828	10,000

That out of every 100 settlers, 95 were men and only 5 were women.

One of the especially significant facts shown in Chandler's map was that Mineral Point and the lead region constituted a mining community; farming was tolerated when it did not interfere with lead mining and smelting. Another significant point was Chandler's statement that lead mining was a simple process; and that was true. A man working alone could dig lead ore from surface out-croppings. A team of two or three men with virtually no capital could sink a shaft four or five feet square, fix wooden cribbing to prevent cave-in until solid limestone was reached, dig down twenty to forty feet, then drift tunnels north and south in order to strike the lead veins which usually ran east and west. Pillars of live rock were left at intervals to support the roofs of the tunnels. The equipment was an ordinary two-handled crankshaft, fixed upon posts set on a wooden frame laid at the opening of the shaft. A stout rope was attached to the crankshaft so that a heavy wooden tub bound with iron hoops could be lowered and raised to remove earth, shale, limestone and finally (the miners hoped and prayed) lead ore. The tools were pick, shovel, gad, (a gad is a pointed iron bar or spike) crowbar, hand drill, blasting powder and fuse. The vertical shafts needed no artificial lighting. In the horizontal tunnels or drifts the miners used candles set in gobs of clay which would adhere to a rock wall in any position. The lead mines never became freezing cold; instead they were constantly quite cool and very damp. The miners wore heavy shoes, felt hats, hickory shirts, jackets called wamuses, and overalls of bedticking.

In 1830, the price of lead suddenly collapsed from $5.00 to $1.00 a hundred pounds. Mining temporarily came to a halt and some miners abandoned their diggings and returned south. The population of Mineral Point at this time was extremely fluid; unmarried mining men were constantly coming and going. There was practically no farming; and for those who remained, food was brought in but was so scarce and expensive that all were compelled to subsist on the most meager fare. The growth of the place, owing to the depression in the lead market, was slow, there being no stimulus to immigration. The census of 1830 showed that the white population in all of what is now Wisconsin was 3,245. Half of them, some 1,500, lived in the lead region, and of those perhaps 500 lived in Mineral Point.

The five years from 1827 to 1832 embraced the founding of Mineral Point, its establishment as the chief lead mining town, and its selection as a county seat in the Territory of Michigan. These years were seedtime in Mineral Point.

In 1832 Mineral Point stood at the frontier of the northwest. In that year there occurred the last Indian war on the east side of the Mississippi River.

NOTES

[1] *History of Iowa County, Wisconsin* (Chicago, 1881), p. 655.

[2] *Iowa County Democrat* and *The Mineral Point Tribune*, Oct. 9, 1947.

[3] Directory of the City of Mineral Point for the year 1859. Compiled by T. S. Allen, pp. 3, 9.

[4] *History of Iowa County, supra*, p. 656.

[5] *Ibid.*

[6] *Ibid.*

[7] *Ibid.*

[8] *Ibid.*, p. 657.

[9] *Ibid.*

[10] Wisconsin Historical Collections, Vol. XI, p. 334.

[11] *History of Iowa County, supra.*, p. 658.

[12] Wisconsin Historical Collections, *supra*, p. 400.

IV.

The Black Hawk War in 1832

THE TRAGIC Black Hawk War occurred in the spring and summer of 1832, when Mineral Point was in its fifth year.

Under the terms of a treaty made with the Indians in 1804, and another in 1816, the Sauks and the Foxes under Chief Black Hawk had moved from their ancient settlements across the Mississippi to the west.[1] In 1832, Black Hawk (he was sixty-five years of age at the time) and his tribe became dissatisfied with the treaties and decided to return to their ancient lands on the east side of the Mississippi. Chief Black Hawk believed that justice was on the side of his people, and that he and his braves were rightly returning to the ancient lands of their ancestors. The whites thought that the Indians were merely savages, without rights in the dispute.

On April 6, 1832, Black Hawk and his tribe, including braves, squaws and children, with tepees and other possessions, peaceably crossed the Mississippi near the mouth of the Rock River and entered the State of Illinois. Black Hawk intended to go north, ascend the Rock River valley and join the Winnebagoes and Potawatomies in the then Territory of Michigan. All told there were about one thousand

33

Indians in Black Hawk's tribe, of whom only some four hundred were warrior braves. The people in northwestern Illinois and the miners who had settled during the previous five years in the lead region, spread the word of Black Hawk's return to his old hunting grounds.

Col. Henry Dodge, who commanded a few Michigan militia at Mineral Point and who was a bitter and able Indian fighter, wrote Governor Reynolds of Illinois:[2]

Mineral Point, May 8, 1832

HIS EXCELLENCY, JOHN REYNOLDS:

Dear Sir:

The exposed situation of the settlements of the mining district, to the attacks of the Indian enemy, makes it a matter of deep and vital interest to us that we should be apprised of the movements of the mounted men under your Excellency's immediate command. Black Hawk and his band, it is stated by the latest advices we have had on this subject, was to locate himself above Dixon's Ferry, on Rock River. Should the mounted men under your command make an attack on that party, we would be in great danger here; for, should you defeat Black Hawk, the retreat would be on our settlements. There are now collected, within twenty miles above our settlements, about two hundred Winnebagoes, and, should the Sauks be forced into the Winnebago country, many of the wavering of that nation would unite with the hostile Sauks. I have no doubt it is part of the policy of this banditti to unite themselves as well with the Potawatomies and Winnebagoes. It is absolutely important to the safety of the country, that the people here should be apprised of the intended movements of your army. Could you detach a part of your command across the Rock River, you would afford our settlement immediate protection, and we would promptly unite with you with such a mounted force as we could bring into the field. Judge Gentry, Col. Moore and James P. Cox, Esq. will wait on your Excellency, and receive your answer.

I am, sir, with respect and esteem, your obedient servant,

HENRY DODGE, *Commanding Michigan Militia.*

34

On the same day, after writing Governor Reynolds, Col. Dodge collected a party of settlers and miners at Mineral Point and went due south to Apple River, Illinois, and beyond where he discovered the trail of Black Hawk and his tribe. Col. Dodge and his party returned immediately to Mineral Point, alarmed the scattered inhabitants of the mining country and advised them to build forts and stockades for their protection. Their fears and the alarms were justified.

The first engagement occurred on May 14, 1832, in Illinois. Two battalions of militia under the temporary command of Major Stillman fought with Black Hawk at a point 40 miles north of Dixon, Illinois. Black Hawk, with only 40 of his braves, put Major Stillman's two battalions to rout. Black Hawk had no casualties. Major Stillman had nine killed and five wounded and his two battalions retreated in terror and disorder 40 miles south towards Dixon.[3] On the day following the skirmish, Chief Black Hawk visited Major Stillman's deserted camp and found much needed arms, ammunition and provisions. The Indians then began to wage war in accordance with their savage customs, scalping and butchering the settlers and their families. They scattered small war parties over northern Illinois and across the state line to the north. They hid in every grove, waylaid every road, hung around every settlement, ambushed every band of white men. They waged savage Indian warfare at the frontier in what was then Michigan Territory and is now Southern Wisconsin.[4]

At Mineral Point the miners and militia quickly prepared for Indian warfare and started to build Fort

Jackson, so named by Mrs. Hood in honor of President Jackson. It stood at the intersection of Commerce Street and Jerusalem Street (now Fountain Street) and faced in an easterly direction towards the Mineral Point hill. The work began by the digging of a trench around an outlined area. As lumber was scarce, the citizens tore down the log jail, sharpened the logs, stuck them in the trench. (The Federal Government later paid Iowa County $18.80 for the lumber.) Block houses and openings were constructed at the northwest corner and at the southeast corner. Inside the stockade, the settlers constructed several cabins for the garrison and their families. The men in the fort, assisted by their wives, proceeded to make bullets out of the plentiful lead in the immediate vicinity. They stored water in barrels to be ready for a siege. As the preparations for Indian warfare were completed, Mineral Point found itself levelled to the ground except for three buildings. All the wood had been used for Fort Jackson.

Mineral Point itself, being the county seat and the capital of the lead region, was surrounded by forts. During the late spring and early summer of 1832, the men in the mining settlements hastily built:

Fort Jackson	Mineral Point
Fort Defiance	Mineral Point (4 miles south)
Fort Union	Mineral Point (5 miles north at Col. Dodge's residence)
Fort Hamilton	Wiota (20 miles southeast of Mineral Point)
Fort Napolean	Diamond Grove (3 miles west of Mineral Point).

A total of probably fifteen forts or blockhouses were erected at various settlements in the lead mining region. In addition to Fort Jackson in the center of Mineral Point, Fort Hamilton at Wiota, on the Pecatonica, twenty miles south and east of Mineral Point was of special interest. Fort Hamilton had been established by William S. Hamilton (1797-1850), the fifth son of Alexander Hamilton, America's great Federalist statesman. The officers at Fort Jackson included Captain Moore, Captain Gentry and Lieut. Davidson. At Fort Defiance, the officer in charge was Captain Robert C. Hoard.[5]

During the last two weeks of May, 1832, and the first two weeks of June, fear spread through Mineral Point and the surrounding settlements. Mines were abandoned, houses deserted, mail service suspended; and there was danger of famine. As the war moved closer to Mineral Point, the women took courage from the words spoken by Mrs. Dodge: "My husband and my sons are between me and the Indians. I am safe as long as they live."

On June 14, 1832, a band of Indians scalped and killed four or five white settlers near Fort Hamilton. On June 16, 1832, a riderless horse splattered with blood ran into the stockade of Fort Hamilton. A detachment of twenty-nine men went out and found the bloody body of a German immigrant named Apfel. The detachment searched for the Indians, overtook them and fought a skirmish which became known as the "Battle of the Pecatonica." Col. Dodge commanded the militia. In his official report, dated June 18, 1832, Col. Dodge wrote this descriptive account:

"They (the Indians) retreated through a thicket of undergrowth, almost impassable for horsemen, and scattered, to prevent our trailing them. Finding we had an open prairie around the thicket, I dispatched part of my men to look for the trail of the Indians in the open ground while I formed as large a front as possible, to strike the trail, which we soon found in the open ground. After running our horses about two miles, we saw them about a half mile ahead trotting along at their ease. They were making for the low ground, where it would be difficult for us to pursue them on horseback. Two of the small streams we had to cross had such steep banks as to oblige us to dismount and jump our horses down them, and force our way over the best way we could. This delay again gave the Indians the start, but the men being eager in the pursuit, I gained on them rapidly. They were directing their course to a bend of the Pecatonica, covered with a deep swamp, which they reached before I could cross that stream, owing to the steepness of the banks and the depth of the water. After crossing the Pecatonica to the open ground, I dismounted my command, linked my horses and left four men in charge of them, and sent four men in different directions, to watch the movements of the Indians, if they should attempt to swim the Pecatonica. They were placed on high points, that would give them a complete view of the enemy, should they attempt to retreat. I formed my men on foot, at open order, and at trailed arms we proceeded through the swamp to some timber and undergrowth, where I expected to find the enemy. When I found the trail, I knew they were close at hand. They had got close to the edge of the lake, where the bank was about six feet high, which was a complete breastwork for them. They commenced to fire, when three of my men fell, two dangerously wounded, one severely, but not dangerously. I instantly ordered a charge on them made by eighteen men, which was promptly obeyed. The Indians being under the bank, our guns were brought within ten or fifteen feet of them, before we could fire on them. Their party consisted of thirteen men; eleven men were killed on the spot, and the remaining two were killed in crossing the lake, so they were left without one, to carry the news to their friends. The volunteers under my command behaved with great gallantry; it would be impossible for me to discriminate among them. At the word 'charge!' the men

38

rushed forward, and literally shot the Indians to pieces. We were Indians and whites, on a piece of ground not to exceed sixty feet square." [6]

From the foregoing report and from facts learned afterwards, there were seventeen Sauk Indians in the "battle," all of whom were killed. Col. Dodge had three men killed and one wounded. Black Hawk lost that entire band but did not receive word that his party of Sauk braves had all been killed until the war ended. [7]

The main body of the Indians, under Chief Black Hawk himself, moved from northern Illinois up the Rock River valley to the north, across the state line, westwardly to the Four Lakes area and Lake Koshkonong, then westwardly almost to the Wisconsin River. A thousand army regulars under Gen. Henry Atkinson plus a band of miners under Col. Dodge followed the Indians relentlessly. After small skirmishes, the decisive engagement took place on July 21, 1832, about thirty-five miles northeast of Mineral Point on the east bank of the Wisconsin River. Black Hawk and fifty of his braves held off the army regulars and the miners, while the remaining braves, the old men, the women, and the children crossed the river to the right bank and retreated westwardly.

Lieut. Jefferson Davis (the same man who a generation later was President of the Confederate States) wrote: "Had it been performed by white men, it would have been immortalized as one of the most splendid achievements in military history." This engagement became known as the Battle of Wisconsin Heights.

The army and the miners moved west along the left bank of the Wisconsin River and established a temporary position at Blue Mounds where the miners, being near their homes, were dismissed. The army continued west into Iowa County, and rendezvoused at the deserted village of Helena, thirty miles north of Mineral Point. A participant reported "that on the twenty-fifth (of July, 1832) we took up the line of march for Helena, on the Wisconsin River, where we intended to cross, again to take up the pursuit against the enemy. Accordingly we got to this place on the 26th where we found Gen. Posey with his brigades, busily employed in making rafts to cross on . . . . This once bid fair to be a prosperous place; there were some tolerable good pine buildings that had been put up; the logs had been hewn, and, of course, were very light. So this deserted village was pulled down, and converted into rafts for the army to cross on . . . ." [8] Among the officers of the army were several who later became famous, Col. Zachary Taylor and Lt. Albert Sidney Johnson. One army officer, Capt. Abraham Lincoln, served in the pursuit of Black Hawk almost as far as the Four Lakes region.

After the army crossed the Wisconsin River, it pursued Black Hawk towards the Mississippi. The whites found much evidence that the Sauks and Foxes suffered severely from starvation and illness. The Indians tried to live off roots, the bark of trees and horseflesh. The final battle occurred in August, 1832, while the Indians tried to cross the Mississippi to the west. The braves, squaws and children were shot without mercy by the whites on the shore and by the fire from the gun-boat "Warrior." It mounted two guns.[9]

The route of Black Hawk from beginning to end formed a great crescent. It began where the Rock River empties into the Mississippi; ascended the Rock River Valley; went west to the Mississippi River above Prairie du Chien.

There was never a hostile shot fired at or from Fort Jackson. Mineral Point and its surrounding settlements were enveloped by the war but saved from direct attack by the victory of Gen. Dodge on the banks of the Pecatonica, only sixteen miles away as the crow flies. This battle saved Mineral Point from Indian raids and massacres. Chief Black Hawk himself said: "If it had not been for that chief, Dodge, the hairy face, I could easily have whipped the whites. I could have gone anywhere my people pleased, in the mining country." [10]

The Black Hawk War lasted during the five months from April to August, 1832. The whites lost about two hundred and fifty lives in the various engagements and in the butchering of the settlers; additional lives were lost in an epidemic of cholera. The Indians lost about eight hundred and fifty out of their total band of about one thousand. The Indians were forever driven west of the Mississippi; the lead mining region was forever free of Indian uprisings.

Black Hawk and his braves were vanquished, but one hundred and twenty-seven years later the United States Indian Claims Commission announced that the then remaining Winnebago Indians were in justice entitled to compensation, because the United States had taken over three million acres of land in southwestern Wisconsin and northwestern Illinois at a few cents per acre and resold the same to the white man at a much higher price, and had failed to live up to the purchase agreement.

The claims of the Sauks and Foxes for sixteen million acres of land are still pending before the Indian Claims Commission, and it may be proved, as claimed, that when the Indians ceded the lands the Sauk braves were not informed of the value of the land, did not understand what they were signing, and were intoxicated by "fire water" furnished by the whites.

The lands from which the ill-fated Indians had been brutally driven would soon be filled by Yankees from the east and by immigrants from the British Isles and from Europe. The situation was typical and was well described by Rev. Mazzuchelli:

"As soon as the savages leave the country which they have ceded to the Government, many citizens of the Republic hasten thither for the purpose of taking possession of the most fertile and attractive places. No permission is required for this, because Government land, so long as it is not sold, is considered the property of whoever is cultivating it, so far as the use of it is concerned. And since five, ten, even fifteen or twenty years may elapse from the time when the Indians evacuate the land until the date of public sale, it often happens that various sections throughout the country are populated by many thousand families, who do not own one foot of the soil they have cultivated. This may take place in almost every Western State, but especially in the Territories of the Republic. Here is one of the reasons why there are no poor in America, and at the same time the cause of the immense emigration to the West of the nations from Europe and from the Eastern States. They go there to cultivate the Government lands, which are yet so vast and so thinly settled that they can satisfy in abundance the desire of every immigrant." [11]

NOTES

[1] Tuttle, Charles R. *Illustrated History of Wisconsin* (Madison: B. B. Russell & Co. 1875), p. 153.

[2] *History of Iowa County, Wisconsin* (Chicago, 1881), p. 479.

[3] Tuttle, *supra*, pp. 158, 159.

[4] *Ibid.*, p. 159.

[5] *History of Iowa County, supra*, p. 480.

[6] *Ibid.*, pp. 485, 486.

[7] *Ibid.*, p. 486.

[8] *Wisconsin Magazine of History*, Vol. 42, No. 4, p. 288.

[9] *History of Iowa County, supra*, p. 490.

[10] Smith, William Rudolph, of Mineral Point, *History of Wisconsin*, 1854, Vol. I, p. 286.

[11] Mazzuchelli, O. P. Rev. Samuel, *Memoirs* (Chicago: W. F. Hall Printing Co., 1915), p. 257.

V.

Mineral Point After the Close of the

Black Hawk War

EARLY IN September, 1832, only a few days after the Black Hawk War ended, Charles Whittlesey made a trip by boat through the diagonal waterway to the portage, then overland by way of Blue Mounds to the mining country. He reported:

"On the second day we passed the foot of the Blue Mound. It is a high hill of regular ascent, overlooking the country, and serves as a beacon to the traveller thirty miles distant. At night we slept in a Block-House in the mining district. Within sight of the station, a newly made grave lay at the roadside in the midst of a solitary prairie. The person over whom it was raised had ventured too far from the house, and approached a thicket of bushes. Suddenly a band of concealed Indians sprang upon him, with the fatal whoop on their tongues; his scalp, heart, and most of his flesh, were soon stripped from the body, and a savage dance performed about the remains.

The country is still prairie, with scattering tufts of inferior timber. The huts of the miners had been deserted on account of the difficulties now terminated, and the business of making lead was about to recommence. Occasionally a farm might be seen running out from an island of timber, and supplied with comfortable buildings. But most of the improvements were of a temporary nature, consisting of a lead furnace and the cabins adjacent. The process of reducing lead ore is very simple and rapid. The furnace is a face wall, about two feet thick, located upon a gentle slope of the ground, with an arch or passage through the center; on each side of the arched opening, and in the rear or uphill side, two wing walls run out transversely to the face wall, between which the wood is laid. The ore is placed upon it, and a continual fire kept up. The lead gradually separates from the dross, and runs into a cavity in front of the arch.

The "Mining District" east of the Mississippi, must include ten thousand square miles. Galena or lead ore is found in veins or threads, more often in a square form, of various sizes, and running in all directions with the horizon. They are liable to disappear suddenly, to enlarge and diminish in size, to combine with other materials, rendering the operations of mining very uncertain. Their course is generally straight and not curved, seldom exceeding a foot in breadth. The analysis yields 85 to 90 per cent of lead, of which the first smelting of the furnace extracts about 75 per cent. It requires skill and experience to discover the vein, but very little of either to work it when discovered. The limestone formation of Green Bay and Lake Michigan extends to this region, embracing copper ore at "Mineral Point," and at other places. At this time the government leased the ground to practical miners, who rendered a proportion of the product in kind. In consequence of the derangements of the times, although the supply was small, lead was then dull at three cents per pound. The supply appears to be inexhaustible. In one respect, this region differs from the mineral regions of other countries. There are but few veins that justify a pursuit to great depths, and although they are very numerous, the pits and trenches are easily filled up, and the rich soil left capable of cultivation. The great drawback upon the agricultural prospect of the Mining District, arises from the consumption of the little timber that grows there, in melting the lead." [1]

The lead miners, immediately after the close of the Black Hawk War, dropped their rifles, took up their picks, gads and drills and went on with their work. The area that is now High Street soon became dotted with miners' pits.[2] The miners tore Fort Jackson down and used the wood to fuel and fire the lead smelters. Sod huts and log cabins were reconstructed near the Jerusalem Spring and in the lower part of town along Shake Rag Street. Mineral Point was rebuilt as a town of huts and shanties. It had a population of five hundred at this time. The village had for two years been established as the county seat of Iowa County in the Territory of Michigan; all danger from Indians had passed; the price of lead increased to $4.25 a hundred pounds; the infant community began to move ahead. The Black Hawk War had served as a gigantic national advertisement for the mining area.

Miners discovered copper ore at a point about a mile northeast of Mineral Point. Thousands of pounds were mined; promoters tried to interest investors; but copper soon played out, leaving only trace elements of copper in the mining region.[3]

The principal product of the mining region was lead. A considerable part of the lead ore was hauled by wagon from Mineral Point north to the "shot tower" at Helena on the cliff overlooking the Wisconsin River. A shot tower is a device for the making of lead shot. In the autumn of 1831 a few men commenced the digging of a vertical shaft down through the soft sandstone cliff on the south bank of the river. Their work was interrupted by the Black Hawk War but resumed in 1832 and completed in 1833. The shaft was 120 feet deep. A horizontal tunnel or drift was dug in the face of the cliff for 90 feet towards the bottom of the shaft and met the shaft almost exactly in the center, as can be seen even to this day. A wooden tower was erected above the shaft and other buildings were constructed below. The lead ore, after being brought by wagon from Mineral Point and the surrounding lead region, was melted at the top of the tower; poured down the shaft into a cistern of water three feet deep at the bottom; removed through the vertical shaft; sized, polished and bagged; loaded on boats and shipped north or south on the Wisconsin River. The wages of the five or six men employed at the shot tower ranged from $12 to $30 a month each. At first most of the shot was shipped to Fort Winnebago at the portage and thence to Green Bay. Some shot was shipped down the Wisconsin and Mississippi rivers. In exchange for the shot there were received by boat at Helena the various items needed by the mining country — salt, meat, flour, beans, stoves and skillets; also coffee, tobacco, tools and blasting powder. The little village of Helena thrived with the lead and shot trade and had ambitions to become another Galena, but gradually lost out to the more centrally located county seat at Mineral Point. The shot tower and its lands and buildings were later sold for $6,000. It was purchased by the firm of Washburn and Woodman of Mineral Point.[4]

Under the terms of treaties made in 1804, 1816, 1817, 1826, 1828 and 1829 between various tribes of Indians and the United States the government claimed title to the lands of the lead region. Early in 1832, before the Black Hawk War, the government sent Lucius Lyon, L. O. Bryan and M. B. Smith to Mineral Point to survey the land. They ran township, range and section lines and their field notes of Section 31 are first dated April 17, 1832. They refer to "Land hilly, bushy and 2nd rate," with "a few scattering trees of white and burr oak." The field notes also mention: "In the south part of the Mineral Point Diggings which extend about ½ mile north, a brook 5 links wide runs south on a point. The Village of Mineral Point commences on top of the point about 3 chains north of line." They discontinued their field notes during the summer months while the Black Hawk War was raging; that was no time for lonely surveyors to work; the next and last field notes of Section 31 were dated November 26, 1832.

The squatters at Mineral Point must have seen the surveyors at work in the early spring and late fall of 1832. That year the United States agent in charge of the mineral lands let it be known that he would not oppose small scale farming; in consequence there was a little farming in the spring and summer of 1833. The squatters were by this time settlers, more or less, and they longed to buy government land at $1.25 per acre, especially since they knew that the mineral-bearing tracts were reserved from sale and could only be rented or leased on a royalty basis.

How to buy non-mineral land and where? This problem was soon solved. In 1834, the United States selected Mineral Point in the Territory of Michigan as one of its two land offices for the territory. The other was at Green Bay. Mineral Point was undoubtedly selected because it was the only county seat in the entire lead region, then the most populous part of Michigan Territory west of Lake Michigan. Furthermore, after an "entry" had been made at the land office, subsequent transfers would have to be recorded in the register of deeds office at Mineral Point, which was then the county seat.

Entries for land were made and recorded at the

land office at Mineral Point as early as 1834 or 1835. The word "entry" in connection with real estate occurs so frequently in the source material dealing with the early history of Mineral Point that the meaning of the word should be explained. The word "entry" as used in the public land laws covered all methods by which a right to acquire title to public lands would be initiated. In particular, under the provisions of the land laws of the United States, the term "entry" denoted the filing at the local land office, or the inscription upon its records, of the documents required to found a claim or pre-emption right and as preliminary to the issuing of a patent for the land. An entry under the United States land laws for the purpose of acquiring title to public lands consisted of an affidavit of the claimant's right to enter, a formal application for the land, and payment of the money required. Later the patent for the land would issue at the general land office at Washington, D. C.

In 1834, the United States Government established a post office at Mineral Point and appointed John D. Ansley the first local postmaster. The first stone house was erected in 1834 at Mineral Point, foreshadowing a unique type of construction and architecture. Levi Sterling took a census of the whole area in 1834 when Mineral Point was in its seventh year. There were 5,400 white persons living in what is now Wisconsin. Of those, 2,633 were living in Iowa County, Michigan Territory.[5]

Theodore Rodolf, a German Swiss immigrant, had settled a few miles south of Mineral Point. In September, 1835, he went to Mineral Point to enter his land claim. Rodolf described his journey: "We found the ridge road through the timber. The trees had already assumed the variegated hues, which a few light frosts had imparted to them; the wild plum trees and wild grapes lined our path on both sides as if they were set out in a regular park. I never enjoyed a more agreeable ride until we came within a few miles of Mineral Point. Here the hills were stripped of their trees, and windlasses, mineral holes, piles of dirt, rocks, and mineral greeted our view on all sides." [6]

It was in the middle 1830's that the Cornish began to arrive in considerable numbers. By sailing vessel from Cornwall, some landed at New York and other eastern ports, then took river boats down the Ohio, and up the Mississippi to Galena, thence 35 miles overland to Mineral Point. Others landed at New Orleans, came up the river to Galena and on to Mineral Point. They were generally referred to as "Cousin Jacks." They would become the most significant ethnic element in the community.

Like all frontier mining towns, Mineral Point had a celebrated tavern. Its proprietor was "Uncle" or "Col." Abner Nichols, a fat, sunny little Cornishman. It was the "Mansion House," known far and wide in Michigan Territory as the best place to spend a night, to have a drink, to obtain a meal. As host, Ab Nichols served his guests the best liquor and food he could obtain; he never overcharged; he never refused food or lodging to anyone, whether the guest could pay or not. As one traveler, Alexander F. Pratt, described the place:

"We arrived at the Point a little after dark on Sunday evening, and were conducted into a room at the principal hotel, kept by Mr. Nichols, where all kinds of fun, sports and music were going on. Such a sight as presented itself to our view we never saw before or since. It seemed that the miners were in the habit of assembling there on Saturday nights to drink, gamble, and frolic until Monday morning. The house was composed of three or four log cabins put together with passageways cut from one to the other. The bar-room in which we were sitting contained a large bar well supplied with liquors. In one corner of the room was a faro-bank, discounting to a crowd around it; in another corner, a roulette; and in still another sat a party engaged in playing cards. One man sat back in a corner playing a fiddle, to whose music two others were dancing in the middle of the room. Hundreds of dollars were lying on the tables, and among the crowd were the principal men of the Territory — men who held high and responsible offices. Being pretty much worn out by our journey, we expressed a wish to retire; the landlord then showed us through a dark room and opened a door of another, in which two men were also playing cards, while a third lay drunk on the floor. The landlord set down his light, seized the drunken man by his collar and dragged him into the next room, then returned and informed us we could choose between the beds, there being two in the room, and bid us good night. . . . We threw down the outside blankets and quietly crawled into bed with our clothes on, except cap and boots. . . . When daylight made its appearance, we got up and found our room-mates were still playing cards." [7]

So it was, after the close of the Black Hawk War, that Mineral Point was rebuilt and reestablished during the years from 1832 to 1836.

During the middle 1830's Mineral Point teemed with young life, lead miners, frontiersmen and quaint Cornishmen. It was also busy with the United States Land Office and the county seat business. It had unlimited optimism. The population was around five or six hundred; and growing rapidly.

For some time there had been efforts in Congress at Washington, D.C., to advance the eastern part of the Territory of Michigan to statehood and to make the western portions into a new territory to be called the Territory of Wisconsin. This important change would occur when Mineral Point was in its tenth year, its last year in Michigan Territory. The exact day was the historic Fourth of July, 1836.

NOTES

[1] Wisconsin Historical Collections, Vol. I, pp. 78, 79.
[2] *History of Iowa County, Wisconsin* (Chicago, 1881), p. 659.
[3] *Ibid.*, p. 660.
[4] Wisconsin Historical Collections, Vol. XIII, p. 335 et seq.
[5] *History of Iowa County, supra*, p. 474.
[6] Wisconsin Historical Collections, Vol. XV, p. 357.
[7] *History of Iowa County, supra*, p. 662.

*Gundry, Gray and Company's store on High
Street, about 1875.*

The Walker Hotel, 1962 (above left); the Odd Fellows Hall, being used as a private residence (below left); the Primitive Methodist Church (above right); and the Moses Strong house, about 1940 (below right).

Bird's-eye view of Mineral Point, 1872.

Cheese house (above); the Mineral Spring Brewery (below).

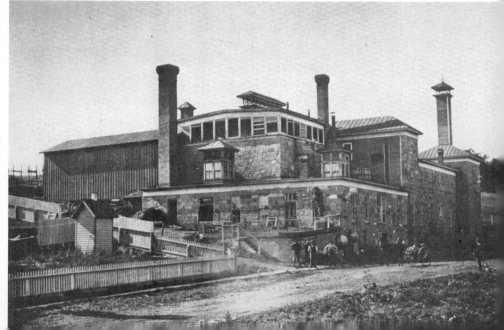

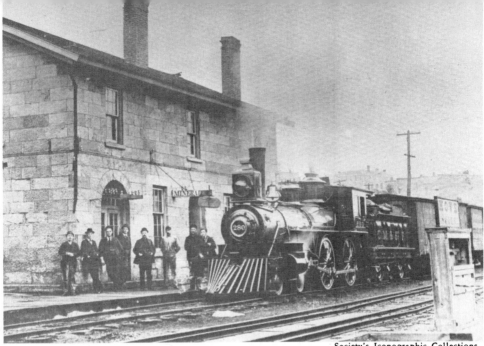

The Mineral Point railroad station, about 1890
(above); the Mineral Point Zinc Company, about
1910 (below).

Polperro being restored, about 1940.

VI.

The Territory of Wisconsin Is Organized at

Mineral Point the 4th Day of July

Anno Domini 1836

BY AN ACT of Congress passed in 1836, the Territory of Michigan was divided and the Territory of Wisconsin was created. President Andrew Jackson signed the bill on April 20, 1836. The new Wisconsin Territory was bounded on the north by Canada, on the east by Lake Michigan, on the south by Illinois. On the west the Wisconsin Territory included the vast Iowa, Minnesota and Dakota regions to the Missouri River. The population of the newly organized Wisconsin Territory was only 22,214, of whom half lived in the distant regions west of the Mississippi River.[1]

President Andrew Jackson appointed Col. Henry Dodge, the hero of the Black Hawk War and the idol of the lead miners, as first territorial governor of the new Wisconsin Territory. Gov. Dodge designated Mineral Point as the place for the inauguration of the Wisconsin Territory. On July 4, 1836 the new Territory of Wisconsin was formally inaugurated at the county seat at Mineral Point. The original official records of the historic occasion were sent to Washington, D. C. and are now permanently preserved in the National Archives.² Robert Dougherty who was a Justice of the Peace for Iowa County, Michigan Territory, wrote the records of the proceeding in script. It would be interesting to reproduce here the script and style of writing in 1836 but it is simpler to give the record in more easily read print:

On the 4th day of July, 1836 at the Town of Mineral Point, Iowa County, Wisconsin Territory a time & place designated by His Excellency Henry Dodge, Governor of Wisconsin Territory —

John S. Horner exhibited to Robert Dougherty a Justice of the Peace for said County his Commission —

Upon which the oaths of office & fidelity were administered as is certified in the words following: to-wit, Wisconsin Territory to-wit:

This is to certify that I, Robert Dougherty, a Justice of the Peace for the County of Iowa, have this day administered the Oath of Office to John S. Horner as Secretary of Wisconsin Territory, also the oath of fidelity to support the constitution of the United States of America.

Given under my hand & seal this 4th day of July, 1836.

S E A L   ROBERT DOUGHERTY
                 Michigan Territory
          Justice of the Peace for Iowa County

Therefore, in accordance with the Official Documents, heretofore recorded John S. Horner entered on the duties of the Secretary of the Territory of Wisconsin, on the 4th day of July 1836 —

On the same day and at the same place His Excellency Henry Dodge exhibited his Commission unto the aforesaid Robert Dougherty —

54

Upon which the Oaths of Office & Fidelity were administered as is certified in the words following to-wit:

Territory of Michigan)
Iowa County   )

This is to certify that on this 4th day of July 1836, I Robert Dougherty, a Justice of the Peace for the Territory of Michigan, have this day administered the Oath of Office to his Excellency Henry Dodge as Governor of the Territory of Wisconsin as also the Oath of Fidelity to support the Constitution of the United States, & I do certify the same to John S. Horner, Secretary of the Territory to be received and recorded by him among the Executive proceedings of the Territory of Wisconsin.

Given under my hand & Seal this 4th day of July, 1836.

S E A L   ROBERT DOUGHERTY
                                 Justice of the Peace of Iowa
                                 County & Territory of Michigan

John S. Horner, Secretary of the Territory of Wisconsin upon consultation with His Excellency Henry Dodge, devised & had executed the annexed Seal as the Great Seal of the Wisconsin Territory emblematic of its Mineral resources —

Price $40 —

On that historic day the new Territory of Wisconsin came into being at Mineral Point. John S. Horner devised The Great Seal of Wisconsin after consultation with Henry Dodge. It was emblematic of the territory's mineral resources. It showed a miner's strong right arm holding a pick above a pile of lead ore. It carried the words "GREAT SEAL OF WISCONSIN TERRITORY 4th Day of July Anno Domini 1836." It cost forty dollars.

On the "4th Day of July Anno Domini 1836" thousands came for the grand celebration. Mineral

Point was acclaimed as the metropolis of the lead region.³ Governor Dodge opened his executive office at Mineral Point, which thereby became temporary capital of Wisconsin Territory. It is probably true that the Fourth of July, 1836, is one of the most historic days in the history of Wisconsin. It is certainly true that the day was the most memorable in the history of Mineral Point.

The three justices of the first Territorial Supreme Court, appointed by President Jackson, took their oaths of office a few days later: Justice William C. Frazer on July 13, 1836, Chief Justice Charles Dunn on August 16, 1836, and Justice David Irwin on September 8, 1836.

Governor Dodge did not select the thriving mining town of Mineral Point as the first state capital. Instead, for reasons never fully explained, he picked a place twelve miles from Mineral Point on the slope of a beautiful mound — Belle Monte, Bellemonte, Bellmont, later anglicized to Belmont, and still later changed to Leslie. (The site is three miles north of present day Belmont.) John Atchison platted the future town in the spring of 1836, and lots were offered for sale at New York, Washington, D. C. and Mineral Point. After General Dodge picked Belmont, there was much criticism and some went so far as to allege that there was a financial arrangement between Atchison and General Dodge, but Atchison signed a sworn statement before Mr. Justice Irvin that no deal had been made, and the excellent reputation of Governor Dodge was maintained.⁴

During the summer and autumn of 1836, a frame Council House and a frame Supreme Court Building, and a few other structures were hastily fabricated at Pittsburgh. The materials were floated down the Ohio River, up the Mississippi, into the Fever River, unloaded at Galena, hauled by wagon to the foot of Belmont Mound and erected. There on the southwest slope of Belmont Mound, the buildings were quickly prepared for the first capitol of Wisconsin Territory. From booming Mineral Point to the new Belmont, one could easily travel by wagon or horseback in a couple of hours.

The Council (13 members) and the Representatives (26 members) of the new Territory convened at Belmont on October 25, 1836. The Assembly voted "that the chair invite the Rev. Mazzuchelli to open the meeting with prayer tomorrow." [5] The next day, after the opening prayer, Governor Dodge delivered an address entitled "Fellow Citizens of the Council and House of Representatives" in which the Governor said in part: [6]

". . . Under the organic law of Congress it was made the duty of the Executive to convene the Legislative Assembly at some place designated by him. In the discharge of that duty I have selected this place. The permanent location of the Seat of Government is a subject of vital importance to the people of this Territory, and I deem it proper to state that my assent will be given to its location at any point where a majority of the representatives of the people agree it will best promote the public good.

Belmont, October 26th, 1836   H. Dodge."

Mineral Point was one of the leading contenders for selection as the future capital but was a mining town and not an entirely suitable site for a future capital city. Furthermore, any land in and around Mineral Point known to contain mineral had been reserved from sale by the Federal government and could not be purchased for the extensive grounds needed for the future capital. Gov. Dodge himself implicity recognized the problem when in the same address he said:

"I would suggest the propriety of memorializing Congress as to the justice of granting to all the Miners who have obtained the ownership of mineral grounds under the regulations of the Superintendent of the United States Lead Mines, either by discovery or purchase, the right of pre-emption in the purchase of their mineral lots at the minimum price of the public lands. By the persevering industry of the Miners the lead mines have greatly increased in value; they have been in war, many of them, the brave defenders of the mining region of Country, they were invited by the Government, through their Agents, to explore and work the United States Lead Mines. This meritorious class of the community have strong claims on the justice and liberality of the Government, that I trust will not be withheld from them. By selling the United States Lead Mines, without a reservation securing the rights of the Miners, they would be deprived of valuable mineral grounds that they have exercised ownership over for years; they would not be able to compete with speculators whose object will be to make a monopoly of all the mineral grounds in this extensive lead region of country." [7]

In this setting former Judge James Duane Doty rode into Belmont in November, 1836. He carried a plat of the isthmus and future city of Madison in his pocket; in his mind was a scheme to make Madison the future capital. During the lobbying and speech-making and voting Mineral Point was a contender to be selected as the permanent capital, but like several other ambitious towns, lost by a vote in the Council of six yeas and seven nays. After the voting was over the permanent capital belonged to Madison; and town lots on the isthmus belonged to fifteen of the thirty-nine lawmakers. Although it is true that no bribery was proved conclusively against Doty or anyone else, it is equally true that the pioneer legislators at nearby Belmont were motivated by their desire to acquire, free, land and lots at the future Madison.[8]

The population of the new territory east of the Mississippi showed the importance of Iowa County:

County	Population	County Seat
Iowa County	5,234	Mineral Point
Milwaukee County	2,893	Milwaukee
Brown County	2,706	Green Bay
Crawford County	850	Prairie du Chien

As to the general appearance of the town at this time we have the record written by Strange M. Palmer, who visited Mineral Point in the summer of 1836:

"The road from Galena by way of Elk Grove and Belmont to Mineral Point, then the great thoroughfare for the transportation of a very large portion of the mineral raised in that region, was cut up and rendered almost impassable by immense trains of heavily laden wagons, drawn in most cases by oxen, numbering from four to twelve in a team. . . .

"Mineral Point, or as it was more generally called Shake Rag, at the time of which I write, was indeed a most humble, unpretending village in appearance, and was rendered peculiarly so by the fact that its few scattered log huts or shanties were principally ranged along a deep gorge or ravine (at the foot of an elevated and most desirable town site) through which the principal road or street wound its sinuous way. Yet, entering it, as we did, near the close of a delightful summer afternoon, at about the hour the miners and workmen had returned from their daily labor, there was in the street a throng of hale, hearty men their faces, it is true, begrimed with dirt;

but with cheerful, laughing countenances, imparting an air of general prosperity and happiness, which a further acquaintance with the place and its inhabitants fully confirmed. . . .

"Among the other evidences of the crude and primitive condition of the town, was the almost unceasing howling and barking of the wolves during the night, around and within its very borders, sounding, at times, as though the town was infested by scores of the brutes, much to the annoyance and alarm of timid strangers." [9]

On July 4, 1836, Mineral Point was a thriving Anglo-Saxon and Cornish mining town; it was the metropolis of the lead region; it was the birthplace of Wisconsin Territory.

The next chapter will give the further history of Mineral Point in territorial times, the days when Mineral Point was putting down its deep roots.

NOTES

[1] *History of Iowa County, Wisconsin* (Chicago, 1881), p. 42.

[2] Letter dated November 23, 1960 from National Archives and Records Service, Washington 25, D.C. to George Fiedler, with electrostatic copies of proceedings covering the period from July 4 to November 24, 1836.

[3] Tuttle, Charles R. *Illustrated History of Wisconsin* (Madison: B. B. Russell & Co., 1875), p. 190.

[4] *Wisconsin Magazine of History.* Vol. 40, pp. 179-183 *passim.*

[5] Wisconsin Historical Collections, Vol. XIV, p. 160.

[6] Electrostatic copies of proceedings. *Supra.*

[7] *Ibid.*

[8] Duckett, Kenneth W., *Frontiersman of Fortune, Moses M. Strong of Mineral Point* (State Historical Society of Wisconsin, 1955), p. 28.

[9] Wisconsin Historical Collections, Vol. VI, pp. 297-302 *passim.*

VII.

Mineral Point in Territorial Times

From 1836 to 1848

THE HISTORY OF Mineral Point during the twelve years of Territorial Wisconsin is the story of life in the lead mining district.

Although Mineral Point had not been selected as the capital of the new Wisconsin Territory, it was an important county seat. It was a booming mining town, centrally located, with trails and roads leading out in all directions and it looked forward with confidence to a bright future.

On December 6, 1836, the territorial legislature at Belmont passed a law entitled "An Act to Incorporate the Inhabitants of such Towns as wish to be Incorporated." The next year, on March 18, 1837, the men of the mining settlement held a meeting at Ab Nichols' "Mansion House" and formally incorporated Mineral Point as a borough. They elected five trustees, one of whom was chosen as president. The trustees met from time to time and passed ordinances for maintaining peace and order; also for the issuance of notes which passed locally in lieu of actual money. Another ordinance established the borough boundaries at two miles square. The status as an incorporated borough continued only about two years, when it was dissolved, probably through neglect, irregularity and indifference on the part of the public and the trustees. The settlement reverted to its unincorporated status as the Mineral Point precinct, governed by the laws of Wisconsin Territory.[1]

In 1836, Moses M. Strong, a lawyer from Vermont, and a companion, John Catlin, rode into Mineral Point and found many of the prospectors and miners living like *badgers* in dugouts in the sides of the hills or in crude stone and clay huts.[2] In addition to his legal profession, Strong was a surveyor and in 1837, pursuant to appointment by the first territorial legislature, he and Catlin journeyed from Mineral Point to the future Madison and proceeded to survey, lay out and plat the new capital city of the Territory of Wisconsin. Moses M. Strong will be noticed significantly in the later pages of this book.

In May 1837, an Englishman, G. W. Featherstonhaugh, who was interested in mining investments, visited Mineral Point. He wrote his impressions as he traveled through the mining country. He wrote a critical, caustic commentary:

"The village of Mineral Point is built upon the edge of a coulee (as a ravine or valley betwixt two ridges is called in this part of the western country), a short distance from the upland containing the suburb at which we stopped. It was an exceedingly miserable place, built there, apparently, on account of a small rivulet, which is a branch of the Peccatonic River. It contained two filthy-looking taverns, into which I ventured to enter for a moment, both of which seemed to be very full, a court of justice being held at this time, which had collected a great many parties and witnesses. We had been referred to these taverns for lodgings, as the post-master had told me it was not possible for him to give us quarters for more than one night; but I was not sorry to learn that none were to be had, being thoroughly disgusted with the dirty appearance of everything; and then such a set of 'ginnerals, colonels, judges, and doctors,' as were assembled there, was anything but inviting, and most of these dignitaries, as I was informed, were obliged to sleep on the floor. This was exactly what I had to do at the post-master's whose house, at any rate, was clean.

"On awaking the next morning, I found it exceedingly cold, and asked permission to have a fire lighted, which was very obligingly granted. Some wood was accordingly brought in, and just as I had got it nicely burning and was preparing to make my toilette, a dirty, unshaven, but confident-looking fellow, walked into the room, with nothing but his nether garments on, and immediately turning his back to the fire, engrossed it all to himself. His free-and-easy way was not at all to my taste, and threatened to interfere very much with my comfort. Under other circumstances, I should not have hesitated to have turned him out; but, situated as I was, it was far from a safe proceeding, or, indeed, a justifiable one. It was certainly cold, and I should have been glad to have had the fire to myself; but I had been treated hospitably, and the least I could do was to be hospitable to others; besides, my barefooted friend had an air about him that imported something beyond the low swaggerer, something that smacked of authority — for authority is a thing that, from habit or from the dignity inherent in it, has a peculiar, inexplicable way of revealing itself. This might be the governor, or some great man, en deshabille, so I thought it best to meet him in his own manner, by slipping a pair of pantaloons on, and addressing him in a friendly manner. It was most fortunate that I acted just as it became me to do, for he soon let me know who he was. He was no less a personage than "the Court," for so they generally call the presiding judge in the United States, and was beyond all question the greatest man in the place. He was, in fact, the personage of the locality for the moment, and it turned out that the post-master had given him his only good bedroom, and that he had goodnaturedly given it up to me for one night, and had taken the "Majesty of the Law" to sleep behind the counter, in a little shop where the post-office was kept, with blankets, crockery, cheese, and all sorts of things

63

around him, and had very naturally come to warm himself in his own quarters.

"The court and myself now got along very well together; he had been bred to the law in the western country, did not want for shrewdness, was good-natured, but was evidently a man of low habits and manners. He was very much amused with my apparatus for dressing, which was simple enough; a nail-brush was quite new to him, and he remarked that 'it was a considerable better invention than a fork, which he said he had seen people use when they had too much dirt in their nails.' He 'didn't see why I wanted so many tooth-brushes.' He 'once carried one, but it was troublesome, though the handle was convenient to stir brandy-sling with.' After a while he left me, to dress himself after his fashion, and a little after 6 a.m. I was called to the apothecary's to breakfast, where the same viands with which we had been regaled the preceding evening were spread upon the table, without any change.

"I had at various periods investigated portions of the extensive western district containing galena or sulphurate of lead, but never had had sufficient leisure to make an accurate and minute survey of the strata, and their metallic contents. Having now with me a scientific friend, and being in a part of the country offering many natural facilities, we agreed to make something like a regular survey, and ascertain the real geological structure and nidus of the metallic contents of the rocks. As a preliminary step, we walked over to what they called the Copper Mines, and found that very little work had been done, and that altogether superficial. Very extravagant accounts of these copper mines had been circulated by interested persons, and we saw at once that they would require a great deal of gullibility on the part of purchasers to be got rid of; my description, however, of these, as well as of the beds containing the sulphurate of lead, will be thrown into a separate chapter. After wandering about the whole day, we returned in the evening to our quarters, and sat down again to ham and treacle. Here it was announced to us that we had to 'shift' our lodgings, as the Court had only bargained to sleep behind the counter with the crockery and cheese one night. We had, therefore, to make the best of it, and lay down on the floor of the eating-room. It was evident that everything was make-shift at Mineral Point, but certainly we found everybody very obliging.

"My berth was both cold and hard, and I longed for the morning. About 5 a.m. a woman walked into the room and told us we must get up, for she wanted to sweep the room and "lay the things," as the family breakfasted at six. Having borrowed a bucket from her, I drew some water at the well, and having made my toilet, came back to the room to warm myself at the fire; but, alas, there was not even a fire-place in it; so I took to walking up and down the middle of the high road to keep myself warm. Not a leaf was to be seen on the few stunted trees here and there, and the chilly, comfortless state of the weather was in perfect keeping with the dismal aspect of the place. At length came the summons to the never-failing repast of coffee, rice, treacle, and bread and butter. Having got into conversation with some of the people of the place, I found that the inhabitants produced nothing of any kind whatever, for their subsistence, not even a cabbage, for there was not a garden in the place, and that they were as dependent upon others as if they were on board a ship. Everything they ate and drank was brought from a distance by wagons at a great expense. Flour, the price of which in the Atlantic states was five and six dollars a barrel, was as high as fourteen here; fresh meat of any kind was altogether unknown; and indeed everybody lived from hand to mouth, without once dreaming of personal comfort. The sole topic which engrossed the general mind was the production of galena and copper, especially the first, upon which they relied to pay for everything they con-sumed, no one possessing capital beyond that which a transient success might furnish him with. . . ."

"I had heard much of a trial for murder that was to take place in the evening, and as amusement and characteristic manners are usually to be found upon such occasions, especially in the western country, I went to the court-house, which was a log building made of squared timber. It was but a sorry ex-hibition of a court of justice, dark, and filled with filthy-looking men, spitting about in every direction. The prisoner was an impudent, ill-looking fellow, of the name of McComber, and it appeared on the trial, that in a revengeful spirit, for some supposed injury, he had steadily followed up one Willard, a nephew of General Dodge, the governor of the territory, and seizing his opportunity, had shot him. The court was my old friend with his breeches on; but, sorry I am to say, he was ill-dressed, excessively dirty, unshaven, and had his jaws tied up in an old silk handkerchief, having, as he told the jury, 'got the mumps.' . . .

"This day my companion and myself, having procured some assistance, continued our levellings, and at the conclusion of our labours we returned to our quarters, where we learnt that the jury had sent a sealed verdict to the judge, having found the prisoner guilty, and that sentence was to be passed upon him at eight o'clock. The court, my old friend, had not arrived when I entered the court-house, and I was occupied looking at the convicted prisoner, whose eyes were glancing in an unquiet manner about the room, when the judge, his person in the greatest disorder, his neckkerchief awry, and his clothes partly unbuttoned, entered the court-room, staggering drunk, and after the most frightful exhibition of impotent inebriety, just managed to reach his judgment-seat without falling.

"I have been present at many rare and curious spectacles, but never before assisted at one so peculiarly and intensely shocking as this; most of the persons present evinced great dissatisfaction, and some of them proposed to lead him away. Leaning sideways, and not looking at anybody, he attempted to address the jury, but he was too far gone even to 'talk straight.' This horrid burlesque was gradually creating a strong feeling of indignation in the spectators, and I thought it probable at one time that they would seize him and duck him in the stream, which would certainly have been putting the 'cap a top,' as the solemn attorney said the preceding evening. As to the prisoner, who no doubt was turning the chances in his mind, he looked at his judge and seemed quite baffled at the probable nature of the coming sentence which the fiery dictates of whiskey might suggest. The prosecuting attorney, now feeling that his own dignity was at stake, addressed him, and entreated him to defer the sentence until morning. As it was out of his power to utter any reasons against the court's adjourning until that time, the attorney directed proclamation to be made, and we left the court, the reeling majesty of the law being led publicly to his lodgings by two of the constables.

"After breakfast I returned to the Court-house to witness the conclusion of this disgraceful affair. The judge arrived and took his seat with that wretched and haggard appearance that individuals bear who are far advanced in mania potu; and, after a few absurd phrases, sentenced the murderer to pay a fine of three hundred dollars, and to be imprisoned until the fine was paid. The disgusting farce being over, the convict was conducted to the log hut which was appointed to be the jail, and as soon as they opened the door to let him in, I saw him make a couple of ground somersets, the last of which carried him into his lodgings. These consisted of a solitary log-house, with one room on the ground and a window with some iron bars. No sooner had they locked him in, than he began to crow with all his might. His numerous friends now went to talk to him at the window, and during the day brought him food and whiskey. In the course of the night he evaporated, and so ended the affair; for as to apprehending him a second time, few persons would be found to attempt that, it being universally known that when frontier bloods of his calibre once inbrue their hands in blood, they entertain no scruples about taking the lives of those who come with hostile intentions against them.

"Having finished our investigations in the course of the day, I began to pack up my fossils and minerals, preparatory to an excursion to Tychoberah. A more melancholy and dreary place than this Mineral Point I never expect to see again; we had not tasted a morsel of fresh meat, or fish, or vegetables, since we had been here. There was not a vestige of a garden in the place, and the population seemed quietly to have resigned itself to an everlasting and unvarying diet of coffee, rice, treacle and bread, and salt butter, morning, noon, and night, without any other variety than that of occasionally getting a different cup and saucer." [3]

"The Court" who was given the foregoing devastating description was Chief Justice Charles Dunn of the Supreme Court of the Territory of Wisconsin. He had been in office a little less than a year.

On August 15, 1837, Mineral Point was visited by William R. Smith. In his journal he recorded:

August 11th. Visited several diggings and a smelting furnace, adjoining Mineral Point. Wood here is worth $6 a cord; coal 12½¢ per bushel. The yield of good mineral is 85%. A good furnace will give 20 pigs per day of 70 pounds each. A new bank of $200,000 capital was established here by law last winter. Stock taken yesterday. The population of Mineral Point is about 400. The town is situated on the side of a hill and on its summit. The streets are irregular, as the building lots are in conformity with the first houses, which were put up without order by the early miners. A number of small hills, separated by small hollows and ravines from one another, surround the town. On the hills numerous diggings are worked by the miners. Some are now abandoned, no doubt prematurely. Labor and industry are not sufficiently exerted. The ease with which mineral has been obtained near the surface has given rise to the numerous diggings over the whole district, and the shafts or sinkings have not been sufficiently explored. Some wells or shafts from 80 to 100 and more feet deep. There is no doubt that if lateral drifts were made into the hills, the advantages in quantity and quality and ease of obtaining the mineral would be immense. But capital is wanted very much in exploring the mines. Several new houses are going up. Timber is very scarce and dear — $6 a thousand is no uncommon price. Pine boards and shingles are here, brought from the Allegheny river, and the new houses in contemplation will be built with lumber procured at Pittsburgh. The purchase of the Chippewa county will greatly benefit the whole country in giving abundance and lessening the price of lumber.[4]

The Territorial legislature at its first session at Belmont passed laws to incorporate two banks, one for Green Bay and one for Mineral Point. By an act approved December 2, 1836, a charter was granted to two commissioners to establish "The Bank of Mineral Point." The capital stock was limited to $200,000, and after thirty days' notice had been given, the stock was to be opened for subscription. The commissioners appointed were William S. Hamilton, J. F. O'Neill, Moses M. Strong, James Morrison, John Atchison, Richard McKinn and G. V. Dennison. These men were to control the organization until the stock was sold and an election of directors and officers could be held. The subscription books were to be kept open six days, and any one was at liberty to subscribe to five shares. The bank was to operate under the management of seven directors. The bank was not to incur an indebtedness which would at any time exceed three times the amount of capital stock actually paid in. If at any time bills became due and could not be settled on demand, the bank was to be dissolved. Voting rights were according to the number of shares. The heaviest buyers of stock were a Mr. Webb and James Duane Doty. Each of them tried to gain a controlling interest, which resulted in favor of Doty, who bought up nearly all the stock at the nominal rate of 20 per cent of each share. The bank was opened in a log building on the village square. The principal business of the bank was transacted with the smelters. Upon the purchase of lead from the miners, the smelters drew orders on the bank, to be paid in exchange for drafts on eastern banks, where the lead was sold. In accordance with that plan and arrangement, one of the first things done by the new bank, on commencing business, was to issue what were called "post bills," which were endorsed across the face with red ink, to be paid in two or three months after date. Although this was an innovation in the plan contemplated by the charter, yet it was not expressly forbidden. The businessmen and the miners, with a little grumbling, accepted the situation, and contented themselves by dubbing the bills "red dogs." The "red dogs" had not been in use a year before the bank began to issue "post bills" for six months. These notes were endorsed with blue ink and were familiarly called "blue bellies." No sooner did the public get hold of them than a storm of indignation was launched. Public meetings were held, and the speakers denounced the bank in the strong language of those days. At one of the meetings, Moses M. Strong made a bitter speech against Mr. Knapp, who had been operating the bank for Doty. That evening after Strong returned home he found Mr. Knapp waiting. Knapp said he had called to demand satisfaction (at the same time drawing a couple of pistols) and that they could then and there settle the difficulty, according to "the code." To this Mr. Strong demurred, stating that he did not care to kill or to be killed, but if, after deliberation, Knapp should decide that they must fight a duel, why, well and good, provided suitable and gentlemanly preparations could be made. After this Mr. Knapp withdrew, and that was the last of the threatened duel. The Bank of Mineral Point continued to operate until the general dissatisfaction became so great that an official examination into the affairs of the institution began to be discussed. Mr. Knapp and his associate, Mr. Brace, heard of this and quickly left town. The following day, a party of eight led by a deputy sheriff, started for Galena in pursuit of the fugitives, whom they captured at that city. Mr. Knapp had nothing when taken except his traveling bag and two volumes of Dickens' novels. Something about the circumstances attracted the attention of the deputy sheriff. He demanded the books and discovered, pasted within the fly-leaves of Dickens, the notes and bills of exchange which represented the assets of the bank. Delighted with the success of their expedition, the party returned to Mineral Point, with the absconding parties in charge. The Bank of Mineral Point went into receivership in 1841 and many "red dogs" and "blue bellies" remained unredeemed. The effect of the bank failure was severe; however, after a brief time, Mineral Point was able fully to recover.[5]

One of the elements that made for economic recovery was the establishment of much needed roads.

Mineral Point was midway between the Wisconsin River route on the north and the Mississippi River route on the south and was therefore somewhat accessible to water transportation, so necessary for the movement of lead. Roads running north and south to the two rivers were gradually established and later roads from Mineral Point ran to other mining settlements in the lead region. However, no attempt was made to reduce the grades over the hills, nor to fill in the boggy low stretches. Streams were unbridged, necessitating circuitous turns to reach the fording places. The cumbersome lead wagons, drawn by clumsy ox-teams, toiled through the region. It was difficult to haul lead ore north or south to the shipping points on the two rivers, but at that time there was no other route. Either way shipments of pigs of lead went down the Mississippi, through the Gulf, and up the Atlantic to the great eastern markets.

For several years there had been agitation to establish a land route, a dirt road, which would more or less parallel the Fox River-Wisconsin River water route. The route through the two rivers was always closed during the winter months. Whites used that route more than a hundred and fifty years, but the Fox River had many twists and turns, and the Wisconsin River was dangerous because of its many shifting sand bars. Moreover, since the Black Hawk War, it was thought there ought to be a military road to connect the three forts: Fort Howard at Green Bay, Fort Winnebago at the portage, and Fort Crawford at Prairie du Chien. Congress appropriated funds, and soldiers from the three forts built the road in three sections during 1835-1836-1837. The plans specified that the military road be "cut out thirty feet wide; all trees less than twelve inches in diameter will be felled within six inches of the ground; and those of a greater diameter within twelve inches; the stumps to be hollowed to the center, so as to retain the rain that they may more readily decay." The road was built according to the specifications, but it was little more than a trail of stumps with crude bridges across the streams. The stumps in particular hindered wagon travel. The Military Road was on the south side of the Fox-Wisconsin water route; it went through the center of Iowa County as now constituted. In 1837, an improved dirt road spur was constructed from the Military Road south through Mineral Point to Galena. This spur was deep mud during the spring thaw and rains, and deep dust during the dry summer weather. The traffic consisted largely of ore and other wagons which were drawn by oxen, mules or horses.[6]

In 1839, a new and better trade route was found — east across the breadth of Wisconsin to Milwaukee, where the lead was loaded on boats and shipped through the Great Lakes to the eastern markets. The new route was faster and cheaper than the old. It took only four days for eight oxen to pull a lead wagon from Mineral Point to Milwaukee, and the cost in the summer, when the drivers could sleep in their wagons and the oxen could feed in the fields by the roadside was only fifty cents per hundred pounds.[7] In consequence, there began a definite shift in trade routes and in a few years the trade ties between Mineral Point and the routes to the south through the Mississippi River were broken and the better route through Milwaukee became firmly established.

A glimpse at the speculative fever at Mineral Point late in 1839, can be found in an editorial of *The Miners Free Press:*

"Here in this territory where money should be plenty and everything cheap, or at least reasonable, the very reverse is the fact. There is scarcely an article of produce, or of merchandise, but a most exorbitant price is demanded for it and paid. And what are the true reasons? It is easier to answer this question than it will be to set people about to rectify their grievances. But all must sooner or later have recourse to that and that only which will ease our burdens — enable every man to pay his debts, and make us a happy and prosperous people. In the past three years we have speculated too much, and since the mania has passed we are a do-nothing people. Many own hundreds of acres of land upon which a plow has never been set, and for which they are every day upon the lookout for a customer to purchase, that they may raise a little money to pay their most pressing debts, and indulge a little longer in their idle habits, which within the last two years

73

they have contracted. We say to them, go to work on your lands, improve them, and raise wheat, corn, oats, potatoes, etc., send them to market, and if they do not bring a high price, take a low one . . ."

The Miners Free Press in its issue of October 20, 1840, announced the establishment of a stage route from Mineral Point to the new capital city of Madison. The stage left Mineral Point each Wednesday and Saturday and the one-way fare was $5.00.

Under a dispensation dated October 8, 1840, or May 2, 1841, issued by. a Grand Lodge, the first Masonic Lodge in Wisconsin took form at Mineral Point. The dispensation or charter was secured through the efforts and influence of William R. Smith. This historic lodge has since operated without a break and has had many members who were distinguished in the territorial days of Wisconsin.

In March, 1841, President Tyler appointed James Duane Doty as the second governor of the Territory of Wisconsin to take office on September 30, 1841. Although Doty never resided permanently at Mineral Point, he spent much time here, first as a Federal Judge and later as a lawyer following the circuit. It was Doty who persisted in the spelling *Wiskonsin.*

In 1841, the United States Land Office was moved to Muscoda, but was restored to Mineral Point two years later.

In 1841, an Englishman who wrote under the pseudonym, "Morleigh," visited Wisconsin. He wrote about his travels as he went along and mentioned Mineral Point. While he was staying at a primitive hotel in Madison, he wrote the following:

"The first morning I descended to the bar, there sat the colonel (the hotel keeper) in his white and black chip hat, set jauntily over his round, heavy, swelled face, his crooked foot resting on one knee, his twisted hand resting upon that, (he had been blown up at the Diggins, near Mineral Point) and his expressive mouth full of a red tomato." [8]

* * *

"This morning a teamster from Mineral Point halted to bait his weary span. Such a favorable opportunity of getting away from the capitol is not to be neglected, and three of our party bargained to be carried away, bag and baggage, wherever the said teamster was bound for. Madison is only three years old, contains about three hundred inhabitants." [9]

The traveler from England referred to the Black Hawk War and the Battle of the Pentacolica (*sic*):

"Many of the actors in that affray are still living near Mineral Point. They arrayed themselves under the stars and stripes, and under the same leader rendered good service, and contributed essentially to the bringing of that bloody war to a close. In that leader, behold the late governor of Wisconsin — Henry Dodge!" [10]

Looking again at the journal of the travels of Rev. Mazzuchelli, as he wrote in 1841:

"This part of Wisconsin Territory is extremely rich in Lead Mines; thousands of men in every direction are carrying on extensive excavations under ground in search of the precious mineral. It often happens that after many months of hard labor, boring through the limestone strata, they find their time and money thrown away. But Providence permits that horizontal fissures are often discovered between the strata wherein Nature, as in a vast store-house, holds the lead in large masses interspersed with clay. Many of these veins are found at a great depth under ground, under water, and while these are usually rich in mineral, the labor becomes so difficult and expensive that the miner is often forced to abandon them. The lands containing these mines are for the most part still in possession of the general Government, but this fact does not prevent excavations being carried on, and all the lead extracted becoming the property of the discoverer." [11]

In 1842, Moses M. Strong played another role in local history while he was a member of the Council of the Territorial Legislature at Madison. There he witnessed an almost incredible event when James R. Vineyard shot and killed Charles C. P. Arndt on the floor of that upper chamber. Vineyard was indicted for murder. The trial was held at Monroe. Strong acted as Vineyard's attorney and harangued the jury while he drank a pitcher of whiskey! The jury actually acquitted the defendant of the murder.

There next occurred an episode which has always fascinated the people of Mineral Point. On February 23, 1842, at Gratiot's Grove, a few miles south of Mineral Point, a man named Berry erected a house and had a house-warming. Among the guests were William Caffee and Samuel Southwick. The two had a quarrel, Caffee drew a pistol, shot Southwick through the heart. It was a case of first degree murder.

Jurisdiction was vested in the United States District Court for Iowa County, Wiskonsin (*sic*) Territory, sitting at Mineral Point, with Judge Jackson presiding. At the April Term, 1842, an indictment for murder was returned against Caffee alleging that:

". . . William Caffee . . . not having the fear of God before his eyes, but being moved and seduced by the instigation of the devil . . . feloniously, willfully and of his malice afore-thought, an assault did make, and that the said William Caffee, a certain pistol of the value of one dollar, then and there loaded and charged with gunpowder and one leaden bullet, which pistol the said William Caffee . . . did shoot and discharge . . . in and upon the said left breast of the said Samuel Southwick, near the region of the heart of him, the said Samuel Southwick, one mortal wound of the depth of six inches and of the breadth of one inch of which said mortal wound, the said Samuel Southwick . . . instantly died . . . against the peace and dignity of the United States of America."

While awaiting trial, Sheriff George Messersmith and the Iowa County Board took no chances on an escape. On July 26th, 1842 the County Commissioners met at the Courthouse at Mineral Point and passed this resolution:

"Ordered, that George Messersmith be authorized and empowered to employ four men to guard the jail at night during the prisonment of Wm. Coffee (sic) indicted for murder and to procure suitable irons to secure him."

The District Attorney was William R. Smith and Moses M. Strong conducted the defense. The jury found Caffee guilty. Judge Jackson sentenced Caffee to "be hanged by the neck until dead." After sentence, the village blacksmith, James James, riveted irons on Caffee's legs, removing them once a week. Each week as the blacksmith riveted the irons back in place, Caffee would warn James to do a good job and would threaten, "If I ever get loose, I'll kill you."

On November 1, 1842, a scaffold was erected in the flat area near the point of the Mineral Point bluff. The day before the hanging whole families started pouring into town; they kept coming in a steady stream until the execution. Many brought picnic lunches and set up overnight camps on the surrounding hills. All told, there were four or five thousand spectators. The scaffold was on the low ground so that the surrounding amphitheatre of hills could serve as bleachers for the audience. There was a spectacular and colorful parade. Sheriff George Messersmith requisitioned Shaw's company from the southern part of Iowa County to attend in full dress uniform, and

Major Gray raised a local company of cavalrymen, armed with pistols and sabres. A home guard of volunteers was organized to stand guard around the jail on the morning of the execution.

Meanwhile, the victim of all this preparation maintained an impudent calm. When the jailor asked Caffee what he wanted for his last meal, he demanded a slice of Judge Jackson's heart. His ride down Main Street and Commerce Street to the gallows was a magnificent show of bravado. At two in the afternoon the funeral procession formed in front of the jail. The company of cavalrymen under Major Gray led off, followed successively by a troop of infantry, and a company of cavalrymen under Colonel Sublett. A band rolled out a funeral march, and slowly the procession moved down the crowd-lined streets toward the scaffold. The prisoner, clad in a long white robe, with a white cap atop his head and a rope around his neck, rode astride his coffin, beating out the rhythm of the march upon it. When the procession halted, Caffee stepped down from the wagon and ascended the scaffold with a firm tread, lounged nonchalantly against a gallow's post while the Reverend Mr. Wilcox read the last rites. Caffee asked the sheriff to adjust the rope "with a good long slack." When the trap was sprung, Caffee dropped and died without a word. The unflinching unconcern bordering on contempt with which he had met his death invested him with a sort of posthumous glamor and fame, even in this country of mining men. For years he was remembered and the day he died came to be known locally as "Hanging day." [12] It was long believed at Mineral Point that this was the first and the last legal execution by hanging in the Territory of Wisconsin and in the State of Wisconsin; however, more careful research uncovered four other legal hangings.[13]

During the middle 1840's there began to occur a change in the origin of the immigrants entering the Territory of Wisconsin. As already stated, the first settlement in the northwest areas was by the French who were historically important, but numerically few. Next came the southern lead miners, moving from Missouri and Illinois to the North. Next came a few Yankees from New England. Then came the Cornish miners, a few hundred of them. In the 1840's, there began a wave of German immigrants into the eastern part of the Territory of Wisconsin, and a few came to Mineral Point. One observer noted that in 1843 the number of Germans who went into the Territories of Wisconsin and Iowa through New York alone was 15,000. The next year in one month, June, 1844, there were 10,000 German immigrants passing through New York, headed for the Wisconsin and Iowa Territories.[14] The Territory of Wisconsin was beginning to be well populated in the areas along Lake Michigan, but only a hundred German emigrants moved into Mineral Point during the decade that began in 1840. The Germans did not arrive in numbers at Mineral Point until the 1850's.

By a special act of the territorial legislature, approved February 11, 1844, the town was formally incorporated as a village under the technical name "President and Trustees of the Village of Mineral Point." The voters were required to meet at the court house and vote on whether to accept the charter. The election was held on March 4, 1844. There were 157 ballots cast, of which 80 were in favor of the charter and 77 against. Later in March, 1844, another election was held and the voters chose a President, four Trustees, and the usual local officials. A village ordinance, adopted in 1844, allowed anyone to kill and appropriate pigs running at large. Another ordinance provided for a "Stovepipe Supervisor," whose duty it was to walk the streets and see to it that pipes projected out of buildings far enough for safety and that such pipes did not come in contact with wood.[15]

On June 21, 1844, President Tyler appointed Nathaniel P. Tallmadge of New York as the third territorial governor of Wisconsin. His relations with the legislative bodies were cordial but his term of office was brief, less than one year.

In August, 1844, Cadwallader C. Washburn and Cyrus Woodman, both of them former Maine lawyers, moved to Mineral Point, formed a partnership and hung out a sign "Washburn & Woodman." In a printed announcement they described themselves as "Attorneys and Counsellors at Law, Solicitors in Chancery, and Land Agents." [16] The firm lasted eleven years and was gradually converted from a law office and land agency into a respected private banking firm, a lead shot manufacturing enterprise and a successful land speculation partnership.[17] Both Mr. Washburn and Mr. Woodman had to do considerable traveling. On January 12, 1847, Woodman was in the east and started on his return to Mineral Point. He boarded a train at Boston; an engine breakdown delayed him one night in Syracuse. He crossed into Canada in an open boat at the foot of Niagara Falls; went two hundred miles by stagecoach to Detroit; traveled by rail to Kalamazoo, by wagon to Niles, by coach to Chicago. He went by stage to Rockford, by sleigh to Galena, by stage finally to Mineral Point, where he arrived in the evening of January 27.[18] Fifteen days from Boston to Mineral Point!

The relationship between the Protestants and the Catholics in Mineral Point was most cordial. This was illustrated by a carefully composed letter dated February 6, 1845 and sent by a group of men who were Protestants and Masons to a newspaper at Milan, Italy, in order to evidence high regard and affection for Fr. Mazzuchelli. The letter was written in English, translated into Italian and recorded in the great Ambrosian Library in Amico Cattolico, Vol. IX, page 390. The following is a translation from the Italian back into English:

Mineral Point, Territory of Wisconsin
February 6, 1845

Gentlemen:

It having come to the knowledge of the undersigned citizens of the Territory of Wisconsin and of Iowa and of the state of Illinois that the Most Reverend Father Samuel Mazzuchelli on his return from his last voyage to Europe purchased the well-known property of Sinsinawa Mound in Grant County, in this Territory with the intention of establishing a religious community, and in due time a college for the education of the young of this country, we think it our duty to encourage his labors by bearing testimony to the esteem in which he is held in this country and to the expectations which this last great enterprise of his has awakened.

Our esteem for Very Reverend Father Samuel Mazzuchelli is based on personal acquaintance and long observation of his conduct as a priest and our expectations that everything that he proposes to do he will realize is justified by the fact that to our knowledge although without means and surrounded by every possible difficulty and privation in a new country the results of his past labors in the Union surpass by a great deal the present project.

The Most Reverend Father Samuel Mazzuchelli was the first and for many years the only Catholic Priest residing in the Territory of Wisconsin which then comprised the Territory of Iowa with a great part of the state of Illinois. In this vast country, from 1830 on he zealously and constantly dedicated himself to the sacred duty of his ministry, preaching the doctrines of the Catholic Church, introducing the practices of his religion and directing and exciting others to erect Catholic churches.

Sinsinawa Mound, the present residence of the Very Reverend Samuel Mazzuchelli, is for its salubrity, beauty, for the quality of its soil and for its geographical position (being midway between Galena in the state of Illinois, Platteville and Mineral Point in the Territory of Wisconsin and Dubuque in the Territory of Iowa, four of the largest and most important cities of this country) much superior to any other locality of these western states for the religious and other purposes to which he intends to consecrate it and under his direction we believe that the most fervent friend of the diffusion of the Catholic doctrine who would wish to contribute to its aid would be satisfied with his efforts and with their final results. We believe that not only the Catholic Church will derive profit from the present undertaking of the Most Reverend Samuel Mazzuchelli. He justly enjoys a high reputation for his talents and virtues and this undertaking of his will be considered a happy epoch in the history of our Territory and neighboring states and generally by Christians and friends of education. For this reason, for the cause of religion and of science, we make this voluntary testimony in his favor.

We are respectfully your obedient servants,

George W. Jones, Recent delegate to Congress of the United States and later Inspector General for Wisconsin and Iowa.

A. C. Dodge, Recent Chancellor — of Iowa, now delegate of the United States Congress.

Henry Dodge, Recent Governor of Wisconsin and now delegate to the United States Congress.

Timothy Burn, Sheriff of Iowa County, Territory of Wisconsin

C. Dunn, Chief Justice of the Supreme Court of the Territory of Wisconsin of the United States.

Henry Plowman, Postmaster and editor at Mineral Point, Wisconsin Territory of the *Free Press of Mineral Point*.

Henry L. Dodge, Sheriff and captain of the Militia of Iowa County, Territory of Wisconsin.

Paschal Bequette, Receiver of Public Funds and Colonel of the Militia of Iowa County, Territory of Wisconsin.

Walter Jones, Receiver of Public Funds and General paymaster of the Militia of Wisconsin.

William Henry, Notary public of the County of Iowa, Territory of Wisconsin, Justice of the peace.

During this period business conditions improved. By 1845 High Street had become the principal street and was the scene of much activity:

"A throng of hardy miners were coming and going constantly. The prices for labor were good, and the cost of goods correspondingly high, and money was plenty, and that in the main, of a thoroughly substantial character. Each day witnessed the arrival of stage loads of tourists, capitalists and miners, who had come either to make, break, or to see the sights in the mining El Dorado of Wisconsin. Speculation of all kinds was rife . . ."[19]

By 1845 lead production in the area reached 24,328 tons. Paint made from Wisconsin lead was now covering the nation's homes; ammunition made from Wisconsin lead was pushing the frontier farther west.

On May 13, 1845, Henry Dodge was reappointed territorial governor; and quoting from the "History of The Territory of Wisconsin":

. . . Gov. Dodge returned from Washington to his residence five miles from Mineral Point, where, after a few days

83

he was waited upon by a committee appointed at a large meeting of the citizens of Mineral Point without distinction of party, by whom he was tendered a public dinner. He accepted the invitation and at the time fixed for the ovation, the 5th of June, a large concourse assembled. The Governor was escorted from his residence to Mineral Point by the Mineral Point Dragoons under command of Capt. John F. O'Neill, where he was met by the citizens of the town and others, who formed in procession and marched to the Court House, where the Governor was welcomed on behalf of the people in an appropriate address to which he briefly responded. The procession again formed and marched to the Mansion House and partook of a dinner which was followed by numerous toasts. The festivities of the day were followed by a ball at the Court House.[20]

The Mineral Point Tribune began its publication in 1847; one of its issues during that year recorded:

"The arrivals and departures of prairie schooners are as numerous as that of vessels and steamers at the largest seaport town. There are now in the vicinity of Mineral Point five lead furnaces in successful operation, each producing about 120 pigs of lead per day which, averaged at 73 pounds, will make for each furnace 8,760 pounds, or an aggregate of 43,800 pounds of lead." (Per day.)

Mineral Point had become a booming lead mining town in the late forties. Its population in 1847 had grown to 2,046.

It will be remembered that the mineral lands had been reserved from sale. Such lands were only for lease by the government on a royalty basis at 10 per cent, subsequently reduced to six per cent. The lead miners had for almost twenty years shifted their thinking about rights in the mineral lands. At first they claimed squatters' rights, or rights of possession, or rights of settlers on public lands. Next they argued that the Indians owned the land but the United States government was leasing mineral rights and why pay rent to the government if the owners were the Indians. After the Indian titles were extinguished the miners were loath to sign leases and sought in every way to avoid paying royalties to the government. In truth the miners believed that they had prospected for lead, had opened mines, had pre-emptive rights, and ought to be allowed to buy mineral land at the land office at Mineral Point at the historic price of $1.25 per acre, or at the most at $2.50 per acre.

At this point it is necessary to record certain dishonest commercial morals among the miners and speculators at Mineral Point and in the lead region generally. Inasmuch as it was legally impossible to "enter" and buy mineral-bearing lands, many people resorted to fraud. A report dated 1843 from the Ordnance Department to the House of Representatives at Washington, D. C., said:

"It is true that the non-mineral character of the lands was attempted to be proved after they had been withdrawn from public sale, by leading men blindfolded over them and then taking them to the Land Office to swear that they had been over the land sought to be entered and could see no indications of mineral. The list obtained from the Land Office at Muskoday during the last summer of the entries of these mineral lands, embraced the names of the highest standing in the Territory, delegates in Congress, Judges, Justices, in fact the most influential men of that region, while others set up pre-emption claims in the same manner as though the land had not been reserved." [21]

The doubts, disputes and frauds over the mineral-bearing lands caused much discontent. The United States decided to file a test case and in 1844 the Supreme Court of the United States held in the decision entitled United States *v.* Gear, 3 Howard's Reports 120, that, "It was not intended to subject lead mine lands in the districts made by the act of June 26, 1834, to sale as other public lands are sold, or to make them liable to pre-emption by the settlers." After this decision all settlers mining lands to which a patent had not been issued were supposed to pay whatever rents might be due and to take out leases for mining. The people in and around Mineral Point became uneasy, but few paid rents or took out leases and much of the mining was beyond the pale of the law. A general feeling prevailed that Congress would pass a law to allow the miners to secure title to the lands they occupied. Subsequent developments proved the miners right. President Polk delivered a message to Congress on December 1, 1845, in which he said that the system of managing the mineral lands of the United States was seriously defective, that according to the official records the rent received by the government for the years 1841, 1842, 1843 and 1844 was only $6,344, while the expenses of the system during the same period were $26,111, the income being less one-fourth of the expenses. President Polk recommended that the system of leasing the lead mine lands be abolished and that Congress pass a law for the sale of such lands. Congress passed a law on July 11, 1846, for the sale at $2.50 per acre, of all the lead mine lands in the Wisconsin land district which had previously been reserved from sale. The President issued a proclamation and the lead mine lands were offered at public sale at Mineral Point on May 24,

1847. Attached to the President's proclamation was a circular which stated:

"The lands embraced by the above proclamation of the President of the United States, contain many of the most valuable lead mines actually opened and worked, which have yet been discovered; and from indication on the surface and from experiments made in digging it is believed that many others equally valuable exist, and may be explored at a trifling expense.

"From the great number of these mines, it would be impracticable to give an adequate idea of their character and location, without extending this notice beyond proper bounds. It is sufficient to state that they are situated in the section of country bounded on the south by the Illinois state line, on the west by the Mississippi River, on the north by a line drawn nearly parallel to the south side of the Wisconsin River, at the average distance of ten or twelve miles therefrom, and on the east by a meridian line passing through the source of Sugar Creek, the whole district covering a surface equal to about sixty full townships. All necessary facilities for transporting the products to a market are afforded by the Mississippi and Wisconsin Rivers, and their tributaries, the Blue, Grant, Platte, Pekatonica and other rivers with which the district is intersected.

"The above district was explored by Dr. Owen, the geologist of the State of Indiana, under instructions from the Treasury Department, and in compliance with a resolution of the House of Representatives, passed the 6th of February, 1839. The above report of this gentleman published in 1844, with the charts and illustrations (Senate Document, 1st session, 28th Congress), contains precise information as to the location of each mine and shows that in 1833 the lead mines in Illinois, Iowa and Wisconsin, though only partially worked, produced upwards of thirty millions pounds of lead, of which those in Wisconsin, it appears, yielded the largest proportion; and farther, that the whole district, if properly mined, would yield one hundred and fifty million pounds per annum.

"Particular lists of sections and parts of sections to be offered at said sale, have been furnished to the register and receiver at Mineral Point, together with maps on which the location of each tract is designated, all of which will be subject to the examination of those wishing to purchase." [22]

As the time approached for the sale of the mineral lands, the miners became fearful that speculators would outsmart them or would bid more than $2.50 per acre. Certainly the lands that contained mines or were known to contain minerals were worth far more than that price. In order to strengthen their position, miners rushed to take out leases and to pay rents and royalties in order to secure government receipts and so have some evidence in their favor.

Many of the claims had been held by Mineral Point miners for almost 20 years. Some of the claims did not exceed ten acres and were bounded by irregular lines. The miners realized that the purchaser of the smallest legal subdivision, forty acres, would almost certainly purchase the claims of someone else. In order to solve the problem, the claimants organized themselves into mining claim associations. Whenever there was more than one claim in any legal subdivision, the miners put up their proportionate share at $2.50 per acre; some one person was selected to buy the entire forty acres, thereafter to make individual deeds conforming to the respective claims. The associations also made arrangements to arbitrate disputes within each group.

The great day of May 24, 1847 arrived. Miners from the entire lead region in southwestern Wisconsin Territory gathered at Mineral Point, probably the largest assemblage of lead mining men before or since. The atmosphere was tense. The miners were absolutely determined that each would secure title to the land containing his particular mine. The great auction was held at the land office on High Street; order prevailed; every sale went at exactly $2.50 per acre to the man appointed to buy for his group or association. A few speculators appeared but when they saw the determination of the miners they abstained from bidding, except in one instance in which a stranger made a bid. He was seized, lifted over the heads of the miners, put into the street, and told not to show his face again.[23]

The miners were jubilant. Many of them and their families had been in possession of mineral-bearing lands for years but without any title. At long last, in 1847, they owned their mines. That same year, however, lead mining reached its peak. A total of 48,290,000 pounds of lead was taken from the upper Mississippi mines and 90 per cent of those mines lay in the Territory of Wisconsin. After 1847, the production of lead began to decline, at first slowly, then rapidly. It began to appear that as a lead mining town the days of Mineral Point were numbered. The existence of zinc had been noticed but disregarded. The miners gradually turned to farming.

The end of territorial days occurred in 1847 and 1848. For a last look at Mineral Point at this time there is a summary written by the biographer of Cyrus Woodman:

"Some villagers persisted in dumping rubbish on the narrow lanes fronting their houses. There were only a few sidewalks, privately built, and the town lacked equipment and organization to fight fires. Fights were common and sometimes they ended in murder. But by 1848 the shifting population of earlier years had begun to stabilize itself.

"Some signs of improvement were apparent in the small village nestled in the rolling hills of southern Wisconsin. Men were erecting new dwellings and new business structures. In 1847 workers smelted lead at five different furnaces, and a new copper furnace began operating in the vicinity of the Point. But though lead prices remained high, more and more of the villagers were exchanging the miner's pickaxe for the plow. The transition was slow but steady, for as soon as the surface veins of lead were exhausted, miners left the ore fields and started cultivating the rich soil of the area. This change, too, affected the Washburn and Woodman firm and somewhat diminished the partners' interest in mining projects." [24]

The lead mining interests centering around Mineral Point created the Territory of Wisconsin on July 4, 1836; the new Territory was inaugurated at Mineral Point; the first governor was inducted into office at Mineral Point; the future Madison was surveyed and platted by men from Mineral Point; the nickname "Badgers" was conceived at Mineral Point; the history of early banking in the territory began at Mineral Point.

During the twelve years from 1836 to 1848 the Territory of Wisconsin had only three territorial governors: [25]

Henry Dodge held office from July 4, 1836 to October 5, 1841. He was appointed by President Jackson. He was reappointed in 1845.

President Tyler appointed James Duane Doty to serve from October 5, 1841 to September 16, 1844.

Nathaniel P. Tallmadge became territorial governor on September 16, 1844 and served until May 13, 1845. He was appointed by President Tyler. [26]

Men from the mining country held the governorship eight years and the chief justiceship twelve years. In truth it can be said that, during its entire twelve years, the lead mining country controlled the Territorial Wisconsin and the politics of Mineral Point controlled the mining country.

However, the end of territorial days marks the end of the special historical significance of Mineral Point in lead mining, in politics, and in population.

NOTES

[1] *History of Iowa County, Wisconsin* (Chicago, 1881), pp. 664-666, *passim*.

[2] *Frontiersman of Fortune*, (State Historical Society of Wisconsin, 1955), p. 23.

[3] Featherstonhaugh, G. W., *A Canoe Trip Up The Minnay Sotor* (London, 1847, Richard Bentley), pp. 67-84 *passim*.

[4] Smith, William R., Incidents of a Journey from Pennsylvania to Wisconsin Territory in 1837, pp. 62, 63.

[5] *History of Iowa County, Wisconsin, supra*, pp. 671-673 *passim*.

[6] *History and Guide to Mineral Point*, (W.P.A. Federal Writers' Project, *Circa* 1941, State Historical Society of Wisconsin, Madison), p. 95.

[7] Wisconsin Historical Collections, Vol. 13, p. 313.

[8] "Morley", A Merry Briton in Pioneer Wisconsin (London, 1842. The State Historical Society of Wisconsin, 1950), p. 17.

[9] *Ibid.*, p. 23.

[10] *Ibid.*, p. 55.

[11] Mazzuchelli, O. P., Rev. Samuel, *Memoirs* (Chicago: W. F. Hall Printing Co., 1915), p. 278.

[12] History and Guide to Mineral Point, *supra*, pp. 104, 105.

[13] Wisconsin Magazine of History, Vol. 42, p. 6.

[14] Inama, Rev. Adelbert, Letters, Translated from the German, State Historical Society of Wisconsin. The Antes Press, Evansville, Wisconsin, p. 48.

[15] *History of Iowa County, Wisconsin, supra*, p. 681.

[16] Garry, Larry, *Westernized Yankee, The Story of Cyrus Woodman* (Madison: State Historical Society of Wisconsin), p. 47.

[17] *Ibid.*, p. 128.

[18] *Ibid.*, p. 61.

[19] *History of Iowa County, Wisconsin, supra*, p. 681.

[20] Strong, Moses M., *History of the Wisconsin Territory*, p. 480.

[21] Usher, *Wisconsin*, Vol. 1, p. 135.

[22] *History of Wisconsin Territory, supra*, p. 549.

[23] Wisconsin Historical Collections, Vol. 15, p. 382.

[24] *Westernized Yankee*, *supra*, p. 64.

[25] Wisconsin Blue Book, 1911, p. 527.

[26] Bench and Bar of Wisconsin, p. 116. Nathaniel P. Tallmadge was born at Chatham, N. Y., on February 8, 1795, was graduated from Union College, was admitted to the bar in 1818, was U. S. Senator from New York from 1833 to 1844, moved to Wisconsin when he was appointed Territorial Governor by President Tyler on June 21, 1844. His great-grandson, Edward Tallmadge, of Milwaukee, is married to the author's niece, Marie I. Amberg.

VIII.

Wisconsin Becomes a State in 1848

The Trek from the Mineral Point Lead Mines

to the California Gold Mines

WISCONSIN BECAME a state in 1848. In recognition
of the lead region, the great seal of the new State
showed a miner with a pick, but additional symbols
represented farming, commerce and industry as well.
The advance from territorial status to statehood made
little difference to the people of Mineral Point, but
1848 is a red letter year in this history, for it was
then at Sutter's Mill in California that James Mar-
shall discovered flecks of yellow metal in the tail race.
It was gold! Within a few months the news had
traveled the long distance to the lead mines at Mineral
Point. One can imagine the effect on the miners. If
they had been adventurous in seeking lead mines, they
were feverish to go to the gold mines, two thousand
miles to the west. How to get there?

In the fall of 1848, three local men, a carpenter,
an ex-sailor and a man with a little money commenced
the construction of a sea-going schooner at land-
locked Mineral Point! The keel was laid at a site opposite the present day railroad depot; the work went

ahead throughout the winter. The craft measured thirty feet keel by seven feet beam. In the spring of 1849 they completed the boat and loaded it on a large mineral wagon. Four horses pulled the boat thirty-five miles south to Galena, where the vessel was launched in the Fever River, five or six miles from the Mississippi. The ship was stocked with provisions, floated the few miles down the Fever River into the Mississippi and sailed south to New Orleans. There the ship was re-provisioned; then set sail without clearance papers through the Gulf of Mexico towards Cuba. While cruising off Cuba, a Spanish gunboat stopped the Mineral Point vessel, searched her, and confiscated the ship for want of documents. The vessel was taken to the nearest port and left in charge of three men of the prize crew. That night the men from Mineral Point seized the three Spaniards, bound and gagged and kidnapped them, and set sail. Once clear from port, they set the Spaniards free in a small boat, while the Mineral Point vessel proceeded towards the Nicaragua River. They arrived at the Isthmus (more than half a century before the Panama Canal), sold their boat to a local trader for a thousand dollars, walked across the mountains to the Pacific Ocean and secured passage by sailing vessel to California. Thus ended a dramatic journey to the newly discovered gold fields.[1]

Other adventurous miners followed the same water route, down the Mississippi, through the Gulf of Mexico, across the Isthmus, and up the coast to California. The mass movement of the miners to the gold mines was by covered wagon, the so-called prairie schooner. The trek went on during 1848 and 1849 and reached its climax in 1850. On one particular day, sixty wagon teams left from Mineral Point. An old scrapbook presented to the Mineral Point Historical Society listed the people who left Mineral Point for California in 1850 and showed a total of 170. In all, some 700 people left from the city for the lure of California gold. Other miners left for the copper mines in the upper peninsula of Michigan. Mineral Point and its surrounding settlements were partly depopulated, business was paralyzed, stores were closed, property values fell, promissory notes went into default.[2]

Despite the exodus of the miners from the lead diggings, the 1850 census showed the following families in the village of Mineral Point:[3]

	Heads of Families
English (mostly Cornish)	311
American (mostly Pennsylvania and New York)	108
Irish	49
German	28
Canadian, Scotch and Welsh	6
Swiss	2
Norwegian	2
French	2
	508

The total population of the village was 2,110. The people were overwhelmingly English speaking and on account of the Cornish were staunchly Methodist.

As to the health of the people at Mineral Point in these early times, mention should first be made of malaria. The miners and pioneers called the disease by many names including "swamp fever" or "chills and fever" or "the shakes" or "bilious fever" and because it was more prevalent in the fall season, it was often called "autumnal fever." The anopheles mosquitoes carried malaria but medical science had not yet discovered this fact. The medical profession held to the theory that decaying vegetation in the autumn and the vapors arising from a low state of water in the swamps and streams were the unavoidable causes of malaria. The settlers thought that the disease was due to people moving into a new climatic condition or to the breaking open of virgin land. Malaria was seldom fatal but it did make life miserable for the victim. The symptoms were yawning, stretching, lassitude, blueness of the fingernails, increasingly severe chills. After an hour or so warmth returned, followed by raging fever and racking head pains. At Mineral Point a local doctor gave as his opinion that people who lived near the stream below the town were subject to autumnal fever, from which the other inhabitants of the town were not entirely exempt. It was an age of medical quackery, and many of the remedies prescribed were bleeding, emetics, cathartics, dousing with cold water, and even calomel. Although quinine was not a cure its beneficent effects were gradually understood, at least in alleviating the worst sufferings. After a time, malaria practically disappeared from Wisconsin.[4]

Cholera, a disease of filth, was brought by immigrants from Europe to eastern seaports and to New Orleans and was carried by the people to the interior of this continent. The plague of cholera was a dreaded scourge. Although there were epidemics in 1832 and 1834, the worst visitations came during the summers from 1849 to 1854. The symptoms were fluttering sensations in the heart, dizziness, headaches, cramps in the legs, a creeping coldness, fever. As the disease progressed, vomiting became severe, and the victim acquired an insatiable thirst for cold water. During the last stages of a fatal case all the symptoms became aggravated, spasms were severe, the fingers and toes turned blue or black and the sufferings of the patient made him indifferent to the fate of death. Cholera was dramatic in its suddenness in that a man could be well today and dead and buried on the following day.

The medical profession at first blamed "atmospheric" conditions and held that cholera was not contagious, but the general public did not concur. Mineral Point at this time had no indoor plumbing. The common bucket with dipper served as the water drinking pail, making it almost certain that if one member of the household came down with cholera the others would soon be infected by the same germs. Furthermore, the methods of disposing of human wastes were of the crudest and many houses did not even have outdoor privies. There were no screens on windows and doors; flies would flit from filth in one house to food on the table in the next. People fled from the plague, spreading it even wider. At Mineral Point, some residents hit on a temporary solution when they camped on a hillside during the worst days of an epidemic. In a letter dated September 17, 1849, a resident of Mineral Point wrote that although his own family was healthy, "We have had the cholera in this village for the last two or three months and perhaps some thirty or more have died with it. There were four or five deaths from it, I think, last week."

As to the cure, even reputable and conservative doctors resorted to bleeding and advised against giving the patient any water to drink. Quacks sold patent medicines and in many cases prescribed calomel, laudanum, morphine, turpentine and sulphur. During one of the cholera epidemics an event proved significant. Joseph Schafer (at one time director of the Wisconsin Historical Society) stated that his mother had been stricken with cholera at Mineral Point and was ordered by her doctor not to drink water. One day when the woman who cared for Mrs. Schafer left the room, the latter noticed a large dipper of water on a chair. Mrs. Schafer "sprang out of bed, seized the dipper, and drained it to the last drop. Then she got well." In due course doctors learned not to dehydrate by bleeding and not to refuse water to the patient with an insatiable thirst.

As time went on the doctors and the general public realized the vital importance of sanitation and Mineral Point got what was probably the first complete cleanup of its streets, alleys and lots. On May 8, 1851, the local doctors organized a board of health.[5]

In the early 1850's the great influx of immigrants from Europe increased steadily year by year. Whereas the first permanent settlers had come from the south, up the river to Galena and overland to Mineral Point, the latter arrivals traveled through the Great Lakes to Milwaukee and on to Mineral Point. John Adam Amberg settled at Mineral Point in November, 1852. He wrote:[6]

". . . on November first, 1852, left Milwaukee by rail to Whitewater, to which point only the railroad had been finished; then by stage to Madison, where I remained overnight; the next morning early by stage to Mineral Point, arriving toward evening. It was election day and Scott and Pierce were candidates for President, Pierce being elected. The next morning I sought the men to whom I had previously written, found them at their place of business and began to work at one dollar a day. I left mother and the two children, as it might happen that the place would not be desirable and I would be obliged to go farther. For board and lodging I had to pay nine dollars a month. This was better anyway than Milwaukee so I wrote them to prepare to come as soon as the weather permitted. In the meantime conditions were bettered. I got forty dollars a month. My first employers in Mineral Point were Deller & Boskowitz, for whom I worked sixteen weeks. The second were McKey & Otis, the third Rowen & McCloskey, and then Joseph Gundry. . . . I also looked around to buy a lot, and it appeared to be a difficult matter, but learned through Mr. Geib that a man in Prairie du Chien had some for sale, so I wrote him and received an answer that he would be in Mineral Point in about two weeks. I bought the lot on which the house stands . . . ."

In 1854, William R. Smith, a lawyer of Mineral Point, completed, printed and published Vols. I and III of his "History of Wisconsin." Vol. II was never completed. He dedicated his history to the people of the State of Wisconsin and wrote that he intended it to be ". . . a truthful History of the State to be collected and preserved from time to time, while passing events are fresh in the memories of contemporaries; professing to exhibit an accurate picture, at the present day, of a region of country whose beauty of scenery, fertility of soil, mineral wealth, facilities of commerce, internal and external, and healthy climate, are unsurpassed in the Union . . ."[7]

After Mineral Point was founded there were occasional deaths and it became necessary to establish a burial ground. As early as 1830, a miner said that when he died he wanted to be buried beneath the "big tree" on the hill. He was buried there and so were many more miners, in fact so many that the continued cutting of the roots by the grave diggers caused the big tree to die. Thus was established the first burying ground in Mineral Point. However, it was not at that time a legally constituted cemetery and the grounds were actually included in a plat of subdivision and laid out in streets, alleys and lots. After years of negotiations the village of Mineral Point purchased the plot in 1856, and it has since been known as the Old City Cemetery.

On March 2, 1857, Mineral Point was incorporated as a city, and its organization in that form has continued ever since.

During the thirty years from 1827 to 1857, Mineral Point survived its economic ups and downs, survived the exodus to the gold fields, and survived the epidemics. The next chapter will tell how Mineral Point survived the "County Seat War."

NOTES

[1] *History of Iowa County, Wisconsin* (Chicago, 1881), p. 677.
[2] *Ibid.*, p. 678.
[3] Schafer, Joseph, *The Wisconsin Lead Region*, p. 189.
[4] Wisconsin Magazine of History, Vol. 43, p. 83.
[5] *Ibid.*, p. 202.
[6] Amberg, John Adam, *Family Record*, Translated from the German by William H. Amberg; revised and edited by Gilbert A. Amberg. (Chicago: Privately published, 1934), p. 15.
[7] Smith, William R. of Mineral Point, *History of Wisconsin* (Madison, 1854), Vol. 1, p. 3.

IX.

Mineral Point and the "County Seat War"

WHEN MINERAL POINT was founded in 1827 in Michigan Territory, there were only two counties west of Lake Michigan — Brown County with Green Bay as its county seat, and Crawford County with Prairie du Chien as its county seat. On October 29, 1829, the Legislative Council of the Territory of Michigan, sitting at Detroit, passed an act which created Iowa County, effective on January 1, 1830. It was bounded on the north by the Wisconsin River, on the east by a line running north and south through the historic portage, on the south by the State of Illinois, on the west by the Mississippi River. What is now Wisconsin was thereby divided into Brown County, Crawford County and Iowa County. The Michigan law provided that in default of some other selection by appointed commissioners, the county seat was to be established at Mineral Point. The commissioners met and selected Helena on the Wisconsin River in the extreme north of the new county. The three county seats of Green Bay, Helena and Prairie du Chien were strung like beads on the historic diagonal waterway. The first session of the court for the new county opened at Helena with Federal Judge James Duane Doty of Green Bay presiding, but there were so few people at Helena that it was impossible to secure a panel of twelve jurors. The county seat was promptly transferred to Mineral Point, which then became the first county seat in what is now Wisconsin to be located some distance from water transportation. Mineral Point in the third year of its existence became the seat of civil government in a vast new county in Michigan Territory.[1]

Late in 1829 a mass-meeting or an election was held, the first at Mineral Point, and Henry Dodge was nominated or elected to two offices, Colonel of Militia and Justice of the County Court of Iowa County. All the other officers were chosen and a messenger was sent to the territorial capital at Detroit, at least six hundred miles away by the water route, to request the legislature to pass a bill to confirm the people's choice. The legislature did so and the bill was signed into law by Michigan Governor Lewis Cass.

Mineral Point had at this early time come to the attention of the Congress of the United States in far off Washington, D. C.

For early in 1830, the Congress passed and on April 2, 1830, the President signed a bill transferring the place for the holding of federal court from Prairie du Chien to Mineral Point. The text of the law said:

An act to change the time and place of holding the court for the County of Crawford, in the Territory of Michigan.

Be it enacted by the Senate and House of Representatives of the United States of America in Congress assembled, That the term of the Court appointed to be held, annually, on the second Monday in May at the village of Prairie du Chien, by the additional Judge of the Territory of Michigan shall be held on the First Monday in October, annually at Mineral

Point, in the county of Iowa, in the said Territory; and the cases which shall be pending in the said Court on the second Monday in May next, shall be tried and determined at the same time and place above designated, in the county of Iowa, and the Clerk and Sheriff of said county shall be the Clerk and Sheriff of this Court; and its jurisdiction shall be and continue the same as if said County of Crawford had not been divided.

Approved April 2, 1830.

Beginning in 1830, all the official business of Iowa County and the judicial business of both Iowa County and Crawford County, in Michigan Territory, were conducted in primitive quarters at Mineral Point. The first annual meeting of the Iowa County Board of Supervisors held in Mineral Point on October 18th, 1830, adopted the following resolutions:

Resolved that this bord (sic) do and now have purchased a house of G. B. Cole in the town of Mineral Point for the purpose of making a Jail. And that the Sum of Fifty Dollars be appropriated to the payment of the same.

*   *   *

Ordered that the sum of fifty dollars be and the same is hereby appropriated for the purpose of repairing the Jail for this County.

The next month on November 15th, the County Board passed this interesting resolution:

Resolved, that the sum of five dollars be paid to Pleasant Ewing for attendance on the Circut (sic) Court at the October term . . . and also the sum of eleven dollars to Parrus Scantlin for the use of his houses and his attendance during the Term of the Circut (sic) Court Oct. term.[2]

The court was a United States District and Circuit Court and was usually referred to as the "Additional Court" for Western Michigan Territory. The first presiding judge was James Duane Doty, who had been appointed in 1823, and again in 1825, and once more in 1828. Judge Doty held federal court at Mineral Point in 1830 and 1831. In October, 1831, Judge Doty came to Mineral Point, held court for the last time, decided the case of Brunet vs. Street, then went to Washington, D. C. to seek reappointment, but failed in 1832 when the President appointed David Irvin. Doty returned to the practice of law, and in the fall of 1832, after the Black Hawk War, wrote a letter to a friend that business was so good at Mineral Point he was going there for the December term of court.[3]

In 1833, Doty was retained as attorney to defend eight Winnebago braves who had been surrendered for the alleged murder of white men during the Black Hawk War. Doty made strenuous efforts to have the trial set at Green Bay, rather than at Mineral Point where the feeling against the Winnebagoes remained bitter on account of the Indian uprisings. However, the cases were set for the fall term of court at Mineral Point. They were later postponed, and still later the Indians were freed and the cases dropped.[4]

After four years of makeshift arrangements there was urgent need for a courthouse, and in 1835 the people of Mineral Point subscribed the total cost of $575 for the erection of the first courthouse. It was located on the village square, constructed of logs pointed with lime mortar. It was 24 feet square, two stories in height, the first floor eight feet in the clear, the second floor seven feet in the clear. The roof was covered with wood shingles. There was a courtroom on the first floor, furnished with a table seven feet long for the members of the bar, and with seats for the members of the jury.[5]

Milwaukee County was established in 1834 in Michigan Territory. The Act of Congress which created the separate Territory of Wisconsin in 1836, left the territory divided into the existing four counties, Brown, Crawford, Iowa and Milwaukee. Later in 1836 the first legislature of the new territory, sitting at Belmont, carved Grant County out of the western part of Iowa County, and the most eastern portions were constituted into Dane and Green Counties.[6] Iowa County was being carved up, reduced in size from time to time.

In May, 1837, a term of Court for the new territory of Wisconsin was convened in the log courthouse at Mineral Point, with Judge Charles Dunn presiding. The court admitted several attorneys to practice, including Moses M. Strong.

On April 5, 1838, when the log courthouse was only three years old, the County Commissioners, at a meeting at Mineral Point, entered the following resolution in the records:

"Ordered that Abner Nicholas be appointed to ascertain on what terms the Court House can be repaired, to receive proposals for the same and report at next meeting of the Commissioners.

"The repairs are as follows to wit: Lath and plaster all round and over head below — weather boarded all around with inch furrow lines put on with strong spikes — Batoned Shutters made and hung upper rooms — Ceiling to be matched and walls lathed and plastered with Chair boards — The lower room to be supplied with a good and neat bar and jury benches & Boxes." [7]

The original court records made and entered at Mineral Point were later transferred to the archives of the State Historical Society. These records show that the county seat at Mineral Point was the setting for a large volume of civil cases covering a wide variety of legal and equitable disputes over property and rights in property, and also criminal cases to prosecute almost all the crimes known to man. Some of the cases were appealed to the three judge Supreme Court of the Territory of Wisconsin and are printed and reported in Volume I of Pinney's Reports. Many of the early cases, whether appealed or not, reflected the unsettled and unstable conditions in the mining town of Mineral Point.

In 1842 the trial and conviction of William Caffee for first degree murder, as related in a previous chapter, took place in the log courthouse.

In the summer of 1842, after Mineral Point had been a county seat in Michigan Territory and in Wisconsin Territory for a total of thirteen years, the County Commissioners decided to sell the log courthouse and jail and build a new stone structure. The County Board passed a resolution to sell the old buildings at a public auction on July 31, 1842, both buildings to be delivered to the purchaser on May 1, 1843.

The work on the new courthouse went forward. On May 12, 1843 the County Board passed a resolution for a change in the plans:

"Ordered that Elearer Smith and Michael Cassin be allowed the sum of Two hundred dollars for an alteration and change of structure in the new Court House which is now in progress of its erection, which alterations consist as follows to Wit, a change of roof from a conical to a pediment, a removal of the dome from the center to the front of the building, which dome is to be built according to a plan drawn by E. Penoya for a Court House to be built at Rockford, Ill. The erection of four columns twenty-eight feet in height the diameter not to be less than three feet at the base, a portico ten feet in width. Said allowance to be made as soon as said work is completed, by orders drawn on the County Treasurer payable out of any moneys not otherwise appropriated."

The new courthouse was substantially completed in 1844. It cost $6,150, plus $1,318 for four columns, a total of $7,468. The building was constructed of buff limestone blocks, quarried locally. It stood two stories in height; the roof was a straight pitch with a pediment. The façade was impressive. From the street level there were five stone steps, a porch, noble columns two stories high, a cupola with a bell. (The bell was not hung until 1857.) The courthouse included a jail, constructed towards the northeast corner on the first floor, and was made of hewn timbers, lined with iron plates. The courtroom was on the second floor, in the front. This second courthouse marked the change from log buildings in a frontier town to a dignified public building in an established county seat.[8]

In 1846, the territorial legislature passed an act to divide once more what was left of Iowa County, and the southern portion was cut off to form LaFayette County. This left Iowa County reduced to a shadow of its former size and importance, and, what was far worse, left Mineral Point in the extreme south of the truncated Iowa County. There began to be agitation to move the county seat to a more central location in Iowa County.

In April, 1858, the Wisconsin Legislature passed a law that a proposal to move the county seat from Mineral Point to Dodgeville should be submitted to the voters at an election to be held in November, 1858.

The law was required to be printed and published by the state printer. He blundered and printed the wrong date; later republished and showed the correct date. The proposed removal split the voters of Iowa County into two almost equal camps. The people of Mineral Point and the southern half of the county argued that the county seat had been established at Mineral Point in 1829 and had so remained for almost thirty years and should stay; besides there would be an unnecessary financial burden in building a new courthouse. The people of Dodgeville and the northern half of Iowa County argued that the county seat should be located in the center of Iowa County. The feeling on the issue was bitter. In November, 1858, the election was held and by a majority of only 350 votes, the electors of Iowa County voted in favor of removing the county seat from old Mineral Point to the more central location at Dodgeville. The Register of Deeds made the move immediately. The residents of Mineral Point began legal action to compel the Register of Deeds to move back to Mineral Point, alleging the blunder of the state printer and the consequent nullity of the election. The case was filed in the Supreme Court of Wisconsin and in 1859 it held that the election was a nullity.[9] The Register of Deeds was legally required to move back to Mineral Point. Its inhabitants staged a celebration, which was reported in the July 12, 1859, edition of *The Mineral Point Tribune* in the following words:

"Our paper is a little behind-hand this week, for various reasons, but we think our patrons will excuse us, as by the delay they get the glorious County Seat news. County Seat Question Settled! Mineral Point Ahead! Dodgeville Gone

Under! The 'Pointers' Jubilant! The Big Guns Brought Out. Hurrah! Hurrah! Hurrah ! ! ! Early this morning we received the following dispatch from the Editor through the hands of T. J. Otis, Esq. "Mr. Otis arrived here about three o'clock this morning, and in a few minutes thereafter the whole city was aroused by the firing of cannon, ringing bells, etc. About seven o'clock 'Young America' formed a procession, and with tin-trumpet band marched through the different streets in the city, presenting a very grotesque appearance, making the air ring with their huzzas. Our City Cannons not being large enough to shout forth victory in a manner loud enough to suit our citizens, a messenger was dispatched on the morning train for Warren, to procure a large 12-pounder belonging to that place and returned with it on the train at noon. A delegation of our citizens have gone out in the direction of Dodgeville this afternoon, with the "Big Guns," for the purpose of giving our neighbors at the would-be County Seat a salute. We understand our Dodgeville friends look considerably "down in the mouth" today, and well they may, for that decision sounds the death knell to Dodgeville ambition and Dodgeville County-seatism."

The victory of Mineral Point was short lived. Two years later, in 1861, the Wisconsin Legislature passed a new law to submit the issue to the voters again. The new law was valid and the election was held on April 2, 1861. The vote was 2,319 in favor of Dodgeville and 2,157 in favor of Mineral Point; thus Dodgeville won by 162 votes. On July 2, 1861, the Iowa County records and offices were moved from Mineral Point.[10] After thirty-one years, Mineral Point finally lost the county seat.

The remaining controversies centered on the ownership of the city square and the limestone courthouse. Mineral Point claimed the square as a donation from the United States. In 1861 a committee representing Iowa County met with the city council

of Mineral Point to settle the dispute. The city offered
the county $6,400 for all its rights in the property;
the county refused; further negotiations resulted in
a deadlock; the dispute was taken to court which decided certain issues in favor of Mineral Point. In May,
1868, after seven years of litigation, the case was
settled by the payment by Mineral Point to Iowa
County of $1,500, plus $500 interest, a total of $2,000
for full rights to the disputed property.[11]

After 1861 and for fifty-two years more the
former courthouse was used as the Mineral Point City
Hall. It was also used for religious, civic, social and
entertainment purposes and was sometimes referred
to as the opera house.

For some unfortunate reason the people of Mineral Point had no interest in the historic old courthouse. They were blind to the fact that they had in
their midst an important monument that went back
to the days of the Territory of Wisconsin. The people
and the town committed a community blunder when
in 1913, after a life of seventy years, the old limestone courthouse was taken down, stone by stone,
until towards the end nothing remained but the jail
standing at the northeast corner. Its great hewn
squared timbers, its iron plates, and its latticed iron
cells resisted the wreckers, but were finally demolished.
The stones and the rubble were hauled away by
horse and wagon and dumped. The old building which
had been so important to the community faded into
history.

NOTES

[1] *History of Iowa County, Wisconsin* (Chicago, 1881), p. 508.

[2] Wisconsin Territorial Papers, County Series, Iowa County (Madison, Wisconsin. Wisconsin State Historical Society, 1942.) Vol. I, pp. 1, 2.

[3] Smith, Alice E., *James Duane Doty*, pp. 39, 87, 94, 123.

[4] *Ibid.*, pp. 130, 131, 132.

[5] *History of Iowa County, supra*, p. 514.

[6] *Iowa County* v. *Green County*, 1 Pinney's Reports 518.

[7] Wisconsin Territorial Papers, *supra*, p. 46.

[8] *History of Iowa County, supra*, p. 514.

[9] *State ex rel Cothren* v. *Joseph Lean*, 9 Wis. 279.

[10] *History of Iowa County, supra*, p. 519.

[11] *Ibid.*, p. 520.

X.

The Railroad Arrives at Mineral Point in 1857

Moses M. Strong and the Great

Railroad Bribery

MINERAL POINT was settled in 1827. That same year saw the first incorporation of a company to build a railroad in the United States, the Baltimore and Ohio Railroad Company. It was opened for traffic on a thirteen mile stretch in 1830. That line and others extended their rails year after year towards the west.

During the years when Mineral Point was putting down its deep roots, the miners, merchants and people realized more and more clearly that dirt roads were inadequate and that Mineral Point must have a railroad to haul out the products of the mines and haul in the supplies needed by a mining community. The need for a railroad became stronger when in addition to mining the settlers in the countryside turned to wheat farming.

In southern Wisconsin, the Milwaukee and Mississippi Railroad was extended section by section from east to west. From Milwaukee to Wauwatosa in 1850, to Waukesha in 1851, to Milton in 1852, to Stoughton in 1853, to Madison in 1854.

The miners, farmers and businessmen of Mineral Point had long been convinced that if they were to have adequate communication and commerce with the growing cities on Lake Michigan, they would have to build a railroad which would connect with a longer railway system. Accordingly, the "Mineral Point Railroad Company" was chartered by the Wisconsin legislature on April 17, 1852, to build a thirty-two mile railroad from Mineral Point south to the state line at Warren, Illinois, there to connect with the planned and projected Chicago and Galena Railroad. The charter authorized a capitalization of $500,000. Construction was scheduled to start in May, 1853. Late that month some six hundred citizens met at the Court House and accompanied by the Mineral Point Brass Band marched down High Street and Commerce Street and one mile south of the village where they performed ground-breaking ceremonies. Colonel Abner Nichols, by then one of the oldest settlers, turned the first sod to start the railroad construction.

South of the Wisconsin state line the railroad from Chicago moved westwardly and in 1854 its terminus was at Warren. In June, 1854, pending the construction of the Mineral Point Railroad, a contract was let for tri-weekly mail service by stage coach between Mineral Point and Warren. The mail left Mineral Point by coach on Mondays, Wednesdays and Fridays at 8:00 o'clock in the morning and arrived at Warren at 6:00 o'clock in the evening, three hours before the railroad cars left for Chicago. Return mail left Warren on Tuesdays, Thursdays and

Saturdays at 6:00 A.M. and arrived at Mineral Point at 4:00 o'clock in the afternoon.

The Mineral Point Railroad Company proceeded slowly with construction; it got into financial difficulties; its partially constructed line was sold on mortgage foreclosure in 1856; and the project had to be and was reorganized. The next year the thirty-two mile line from Warren was completed into Mineral Point. That year also saw the completion of the railroad passenger station. Workmen constructed it of local buff limestone, with the courses of stone blocks closely fitted and tooled. The elevations were symmetrical with arched stone door openings.[1]

The route of the new railroad ran southwardly from Mineral Point to Calamine, to Darlington, to Gratiot, to Warren, immediately south of the state line.

On June 16, 1857, the first train puffed into town and on June 30th, the *Mineral Point Tribune* reported: "The business of the Mineral Point Railroad exceeds the expectations of most of our citizens . . . . We were at the Depot on Friday last about the time the train was leaving and saw it start out with seven freight cars well filled, three loaded with wheat, three with lead, and one with sundries."

The original schedule of the thirty-two mile line was simple. The train left Warren each day at 9:30 in the forenoon and arrived at Mineral Point at noon. It left Mineral Point at 2:00 P.M. and arrived at Warren at 5:00 P.M.[2] At Warren the main railroad had by 1857 been extended west. At last in 1857 Mineral Point had satisfactory railroad service to

Warren and at that point had good connections both east and west.

The financial panic of 1857 occurred the year the railroad opened; and although 1858 was still a time of depression, the railroad carried a surprising amount of freight out of Mineral Point:

	Pounds
Wheat	4,591,933
Lead	3,451,559
Oats	1,882,619
Pork	191,104
Hides	78,359
Corn	64,800

In addition the railroad carried out 5,479 barrels of flour, 391 head of cattle and 256 hogs. The passenger service in 1858 provided service for 9,100 persons or about 28 per day, in and out combined.

After the coming of the railroad in 1857 it took only two years to accomplish definite changes and these were reflected in the Mineral Point "Official Directory 1859," published by T. S. Allen. This printed booklet gave an excellent summary of the town's history from 1827 to 1859 and added a directory of all the churches, establishments and businesses in the city. The booklet was also a prospectus which boosted the past, present and future advantages of the community and carried a tone of unrestrained optimism and enthusiasm. Most significantly the history and directory showed that Mineral Point had been weaned away from Galena and the south and had turned to the east with its great cities. The train service to Warren was fully established:

Going South

Leave Mineral Point at	6:45 A.M.
Leave Calamine at	7:15 A.M.
Leave Darlington at	7:40 A.M.
Leave Riverside at	8:10 A.M.
Arrive at Warren at	8:45 A.M.

Going North

Leave Warren at	9:45 A.M.
Leave Riverside at	10:10 A.M.
Leave Darlington at	10:45 A.M.
Leave Calamine at	11:10 A.M.
Arrive at Mineral Point at	11:45 A.M.

A map of Mineral Point and its connections was inserted in the 1859 directory and is shown on the opposite page.

In 1880, the Milwaukee Road purchased the Mineral Point Railroad; through passenger service to Milwaukee twice a day each way was established in 1881; the service to Warren was then discontinued. In November, 1882, the schedule for the morning passenger train out of Mineral Point was to leave at 8:45, go through Janesville and Milwaukee and arrive at Chicago at 7:00 o'clock in the evening. Almost ten hours were needed to travel from Mineral Point to Chicago.

There would be railroad passenger service in and out of Mineral Point for 100 years, then changing times would compel the railroad to limit its service to freight, and would leave travelers once again to find the nearest passenger service at Warren.

Moses M. Strong of Mineral Point was in 1856 the central figure in an amazing and brazen railroad scheme that actually corrupted and bribed the whole government of Wisconsin. Strong worked as a railroad lobbyist at Washington, D. C. and in 1856 secured a huge land grant from Congress for the construction of a railroad to run from Madison or Columbus by way of the portage to the St. Croix River, thence north to the west end of Lake Superior. The grant consisted of more than a million acres of Wisconsin land, a princely gift, and the final allocation was left to the State of Wisconsin. Several railroads schemed to secure the grant. Through mergers only two remained. One of them was the La Crosse and Milwaukee Railroad, dominated by Byron Kilbourn of Milwaukee and Moses M. Strong of Mineral Point. These two men deliberately corrupted and bribed the governor, the legislature, a supreme court justice and newspaper editors and secured the great land grant for their railroad. On October 9, 1856, the Assembly and Senate passed the necessary legislation; two days later Gov. Coles Bashford signed the bill; the La Crosse and Milwaukee Railroad formally accepted the grant. Then followed the payoff. Moses M. Strong handed over $862,000 in railroad bonds in bribes to the governor, lieutenant governor, state senators, assemblymen, Milwaukee newspaper publishers and others. Gov. Bashford was paid $50,000. Justice Abram D. Smith of the Wisconsin Supreme Court was paid $10,000. The Lieutenant Governor, the governor's secretary, the chief clerk and assistant clerks of the assembly each received $10,000 or $5,000. Each senator who voted favorably received $10,000, and each assemblyman who voted in favor got $5,000.

The bribes were paid in first mortgage bonds of the La Crosse and Milwaukee Railroad Company, worth par at the time. Historians and others have long been fascinated with the mechanics of the pay-off. Two lists were made. One contained the names of the officials and editors who had been corrupted, with a number opposite each name. The other list contained the numbers and the amount of each bribe. The bonds were wrapped in plain paper and each package was numbered according to the lists. Strong lived in Milwaukee temporarily and had an office on Third Street. Between October 15 and 21, 1856, Governor Coles Bashford, the lieutenant governor, the senators, the assemblymen and the others came to Strong and each received his bribe.

The secret of the colossal bribery of the whole government of a sovereign state soon leaked out. The whisperings grew louder. In 1857 ugly rumors of the briberies ran through the entire state and the public demanded a full investigation; but Governor Bashford was still in office and many of the legislators were the same men who the year before had received corruption bonds. A committee of the assembly voted against an investigation. In 1858, however, there was a new administration; Governor Randall took office and there were many new faces in the legislature. The people and the new administration insisted on a full investigation and this time the assembly appointed a committee which went ahead. Strong refused to testify and spent six days in the Dane County jail on a contempt citation; he then testified and admitted making the bribes. The truth was finally out.[3]

The investigative committee called many witnesses. Reputations were destroyed despite the feeble efforts of many of the corrupted officials to explain away the facts. For instance, Mr. Justice Abram Smith of the Wisconsin Supreme Court testified:

"Some time in the latter part of 1856, or forepart of 1857, I think in January, 1857, but am not sure, I found one morning on my table, in my library in Milwaukee, a package containing ten bonds of the La Crosse and Milwaukee Railroad Company, payable five years from date, I think. From whom they came, I did not know; or for what purpose; but supposed most likely they were left there by the management or direction of the La Crosse Company, and I had no reason that I knew, or could think of, to believe or suspect that they were intended for any unworthy purpose. But although I stood in no official relation to the Company, I could perceive that such relation might arise. I could foresee other circumstances wherein I thought it would be my duty, in justice as well to myself as to the State, to retain those bonds, safely and securely within my control, to be produced as circumstances might require. I therefore replaced the bonds in the envelope, took them into the bank where I kept my account, and requested the Cashier to put his seal upon it, deposited the package in the vault of the bank subject to my order, as a special deposit, and there they remain to this day." [4]

Although Moses M. Strong by his infamous bribery of the machinery of government in Wisconsin brought disgrace to Mineral Point, the city was at the same time honored by the sterling character of State Senator Amasa M. Cobb of the law firm of Cobb and Messmore of Mineral Point. Kilbourn, one of the conspirators, sent an official who was already corrupted to bribe Senator Cobb but the latter refused. Later during the investigation, Senator Cobb stated:

"Some five or six days before the final adjournment of the said adjourned session Mr. William Pitt Dewey, who was then the assistant clerk of the Assembly, invited me to take a walk with him, and while walking around the capital (*sic*) square in the City of Madison, he (Dewey) introduced the subject of the bill granting the lands which had been granted to the State of Wisconsin to aid in the construction of certain railroads, to the La Crosse and Milwaukee Railroad Company, and which bill was then pending before the Legislature. During said conversation he informed me that should said bill pass, he would get a quantity of bonds. He stated the amount that he was to receive, and to the best of the recollection of this deponent, it was ten thousand dollars. He asked me what amount would induce me to cease my opposition and support the bill, or come into the arrangement. I asked him why, or by what authority he made the inquiry? He replied that he had come right from Kilbourn and was authorized by him to say that I might make my own terms . . . He further stated that they were bound to carry it through anyhow, and that I might as well make something out of it, as the rest of them. . . . I asked him what was the amount of the capital stock of the company? He replied ten million dollars. I told him to say to Byron Kilbourn that if he would multiply the capital stock of the company by the number of leaves in the Capitol Park, and give me that amount in money, and then have himself, Moses Strong, and Mitchell blacked, and give me a clear title to them as servants for life, I would take the matter under consideration." [5]

Strong was never disbarred for his corruption and bribery; and diligent research has not uncovered any move to have him disbarred. On the contrary he managed a comeback. In 1868 he erected a mansion of cut limestone on Fountain Street in Mineral Point. Strong had his house piped for gas lighting and for indoor plumbing. He built a tennis court in the garden. The house, which the family called "The Stronghold," was furnished with black walnut furniture, a rosewood piano, carpeting, and lace curtains. It contained a library which included Strong's law books and several hundred volumes in Greek, Latin, English, French and German.[6] In 1877, Strong's only son drowned in a tragic accident in the Flambeau River; the president of the Wisconsin Central Railroad sent Strong on a special train to bring the son's body back to Mineral Point for burial.[7] In 1879, Strong, as the oldest practicing lawyer in Wisconsin, delivered the main address to the law graduating class at the University of Wisconsin.[8] Strong spent several years in "The Stronghold" writing the "History of the Territory of Wisconsin," which he published in 1885.[9] From 1885 to 1894 he was president of the state board of law examiners; from 1887 to 1893 he was vice-president of the Wisconsin State Historical Society; from 1890 to 1894 he was president of the Wisconsin State Bar Association. He died in his home, "The Stronghold" in 1894, leaving no fortune. He lies buried in Graceland Cemetery.

Although Strong must be condemned for his part in the great railroad bribery, his career at Mineral Point and throughout Wisconsin from 1836 to 1894 spanned fifty-eight years of the formative period of the territory and the state of Wisconsin. The later years of Strong's career, it seems, indicated the workings of redeeming influences in his character.

NOTES

[1] *History of Iowa County, Wisconsin* (Chicago, 1881), pp. 521-531, *passim.*
[2] *Iowa County Democrat* and *Mineral Point Tribune.* Oct. 9, 1947, Section 2, p. 5.

[3] Duckett, Kenneth W., *Frontiersman of Fortune; Moses M. Strong of Mineral Point* (Madison: State Historical Society of Wisconsin, 1955), pp. 127-140, *passim*.

[4] Hunt, Robert S., *Law and Locomotives* (Madison: State Historical Society of Wisconsin, 1958), p. 22.

[5] *Law and Locomotives, supra*, p. 14.

[6] *Frontiersman of Fortune: Moses M. Strong of Mineral Point* (Madison: State Historical Society of Wisconsin, 1955), p. 174.

[7] *Ibid.*, p. 184.

[8] *Ibid.*, p. 186.

[9] Strong, Moses M., *History of Wisconsin Territory* (Madison, Wis.: Democrat Printing Co., 1885.)

XI.

Mineral Point and The Civil War, 1861-1864

IN 1860, after several years of bitter debate about slavery and states rights, the nation, the State of Wisconsin, the County of Iowa, and the City of Mineral Point went strongly Republican, and Abraham Lincoln was elected President by a plurality of the popular vote and a majority of the electoral college. Promptly thereafter, on December 26, 1860, before Lincoln took office, South Carolina seceded and by February, 1861, six more states seceded.

Lincoln took office in March, 1861. The next month, on April 12, the southern secessionists fired on Fort Sumter in the harbor of Charleston, South Carolina, the fort fell, and the nation plunged into civil war. There would soon be brothers and cousins fighting on opposite sides.

Events moved quickly. On April 15, President Lincoln issued a first call for 75,000 volunteers. Only a week later, on April 22nd, the City Council of Mineral Point passed a resolution to pay six dollars per month to the families of the first twelve married men who would enlist here.[1]

The Miners' Guard at Mineral Point had been merely a state militia with sixty members, which after Lincoln's call had quickly increased its ranks to 130 soldiers. The entire guard volunteered for the front and was accepted. A problem arose as to how to reduce the Miners' Guard to a regular company of seventy-eight men, but not a single member offered to relinquish his post. A committee solved the problem by selecting a number of men for home duty. The committee performed its delicate duties carefully and for the most part designated married men with families for home duty. The Miners' Guard was enrolled as Company I of the Second Wisconsin Regiment, and ordered to report at Camp Randall at Madison. On the day of parting, the men assembled at the former courthouse, renamed the city hall, and departed amid cheers, music and waving flags. Wagons conveyed them to Arena where they boarded the railroad to Camp Randall at Madison. (At that time the railroad at Mineral Point went south to Warren.) The men arrived at Camp Randall in May, the month after the fall of Fort Sumter.[2]

Moses M. Strong, an ardent Democrat, opposed the election of Lincoln and argued that his election would mean war. He made speeches throughout Wisconsin which were anti-war, anti-Republican and anti-Lincoln. On the Fourth of July, 1861, in his home town of Mineral Point, Strong delivered a long and carefully prepared oration. It was printed in pamphlet form and entitled: ADDRESS OF HON. M. M. STRONG, DELIVERED AT MINERAL POINT, JULY 4TH, 1861. Copies can still be found at Mineral Point. In this speech Strong summarized the views and arguments he made during the previous months. He reviewed the history of the Declaration of Independence and the Constitution of the United States. He denied the right of any state to secede; he opposed treason; he urged his audience to put down the insurrection of the South. At the same time he examined the right of the people to change their form of government; he warned against the cost of civil war in lives and treasure; he bitterly assailed Lincoln's suspension of the right of habeas corpus. In short, Moses M. Strong straddled, and this was proved in his peroration in which he said:

"It should be the primary desire of every patriotic citizen to terminate this war at the earliest practicable moment in which it can be honorably done, without abandoning the only principle upon which its continuance for a day can be justified, viz: the maintenance of the integrity of the Union against the attempts of the seceded States to break it up.

"Whenever those attempts shall be abandoned, as the result either of the victories or the moderation of the government, the proper steps should be immediately taken by reasonable concessions to, and compromises with the disaffected States to restore the government to its normal condition of harmonious unity, if possible; and if impossible to the peaceful separation of such part as cannot after all reasonable concessions, still continue in the Union."

Thus the heart of Strong's argument about the seceded states was to let them go. Strong was a dedicated Copperhead. He received threatening letters and one included the drawing of a snake entitled Moses Strong — Copperhead. His family urged him to remain silent, lest he be imprisoned. However, he continued on the same path, but with no success. The Civil War continued for four years.

The Miners' Guard, now Company I of the Second Regiment, moved from Camp Randall to Chicago, to Pittsburgh, to Washington, D. C., to a camp on the Fairfax River near Fort Corcoran. On July 16th, they moved on to Manassas, and on July 18th participated in an attack against the Confederates at Blackburn's Ford on Bull Run. That evening they bivouacked near Centerville. On July 21st, Company I was part of the division that crossed Bull Run towards Manassas. The Second Regiment was later consolidated with the Fifth and Sixth Wisconsin Regiments and became part of the famous Wisconsin "Iron Brigade."

Inspired by the Mineral Point miners, the farmers in the surrounding countryside organized the Farmers' Guards, which in October, 1861, was mustered into service as Company E of the Eleventh Wisconsin Regiment.[3]

Cyrus Woodman, the respected lawyer, banker and land agent, donated money to equip an entire company of Mineral Point volunteers. His partner, Cadwallader C. Washburn, also a respected Mineral Point lawyer and the future governor of Wisconsin, was in 1861 commissioned colonel of the Second Wisconsin Volunteers.

Early in the war the women of Mineral Point formed a society to aid the soldiers. When the need arose the women worked day and night. On a Wednesday evening early in July, 1861, word came from Camp Randall that the Miners' Guard needed 101 haversacks. The women purchased the cloth, set to work and by two o'clock on Friday afternoon had 101 haversacks ready for shipment to their men. In December that year the soldiers from Mineral Point were at Camp Curtis, Maryland and held a meeting to thank the women for sending more than a hundred pairs of mittens.

The Civil War brought renewed prosperity to Mineral Point, which was the regional shipping point for wheat, livestock and lead. Abandoned lead mines were reworked and new ones opened. For the first time in twenty years a mining boom swept through the mineral region. Prices soared. Pig lead rose from $4.90 a hundred pounds in July 1861, to $7.50 in 1863, to $15.00 in January, 1865.[4]

The Civil War went on and on, progressively more grim. The first Mineral Point casualties occurred in the battle of Gainesville on August 28, 1862, when Corporal Curry and Private Kay were slain. The first national draft occurred in 1862 and called for 638 men from Iowa County, including 34 from the City of Mineral Point. The final draft in 1864 was a desperate appeal to the loyalty of the people, but all difficulties were overcome and Mineral Point met its quota.[5]

The Miners' Guard had enlisted for three years and returned home on July 2, 1864. They were met by the Mineral Point Brass Band, and conducted to the United States Hotel, where they arrived at five o'clock in the afternoon. Alexander Wilson, afterwards Attorney General of Wisconsin, gave the address of welcome and a choir of young ladies sang appropriate songs for the occasion.[6]

Also during the summer of 1864 a company of the Thirtieth Regiment arrived home on furlough. They were young, high spirited, at temporary liberty from camp, rejoicing in the company of their friends. These circumstances heightened by chauvinism and an abundance of liquor, produced an episode which illustrated the ties that still existed at Mineral Point with the old South. Although the people of Mineral Point were overwhelmingly in favor of the preservation of the Union and strongly against slavery, there were a few die hard Breckinridge Democrats, a few members of the Knights of the Golden Circle, a few southern sympathizers, a few local Copperheads. They had been mostly silenced at Mineral Point by an avalanche of patriotism. However, one exception was Dr. Van Dusen, who remained outspoken in his sympathies. The soldiers threatened to burn Dr. Van Dusen's house to the ground. His friends guarded the residence until the men left.

The Civil War was over in 1865 and the people everywhere were aghast at the casualties. The north mobilized 2,213,363 men and counted 364,511 dead. The South mobilized about 1,000,000 men and had 208,000 dead. Thus the nation mourned for 572,511 young men killed in the war.

The Grand Army of the Republic had an active branch at Mineral Point. Each year on Decoration Day, May thirtieth, the soldiers of the Civil War would solemnly visit the cemeteries, decorate the graves of their brethren, march up High Street to the Water Tower Park, and call the roll of the Mineral Point men who had served as soldiers in the Civil War. Each year the procession of old soldiers was shorter; each year the roll call of the dead was longer. The GAR kept the memory of the Civil War very much alive for at least fifty years from 1865 to 1915. For the Civil War was quite different from the wars to come in that it occurred in this country, it was fought between American citizens, it was a frightful blood bath, it seemed to produce a continuing profound impression, its shadows lasted more than fifty years.

The Civil War and its aftermath marked the advance of Mineral Point into more modern times, as will be outlined in the succeeding chapters of this book.

NOTES

[1] *History of Iowa County, Wisconsin* (Chicago, 1881), p. 553.

[2] *Ibid.*, p. 546.

[3] *Ibid.*, p. 547.

[4] *History and Guide to Mineral Point* (W. P. A. Federal Writers' Project, *Circa* 1941, State Historical Society of Wisconsin, Madison), p. 205.

[5] *History of Iowa County, Wisconsin, supra*, pp. 551, 552.

[6] *Ibid.*, p. 553.

XII.

The Middle Years

AFTER THE CIVIL WAR ended in 1865, Mineral Point moved into more modern times and entered upon several decades of uninterrupted progress. The times and conditions and numerous inventions during the last third of that century marked world wide changes. The city of Mineral Point grew in size, advanced in wealth, built several stately houses, began to be modernized, became extremely self-satisfied and confident. The best building period that Mineral Point ever had began in 1865. The rise of zinc mining and the manufacture of zinc oxide caused a new boom at Mineral Point during these middle years, a story so important that it will be reserved for a separate chapter.

In 1867 Joseph Gundry, a successful general store merchant, mining investor and money lender, built a large and beautiful house of cut sandstone. The surrounding grounds comprised eleven acres and were planted with a variety of native and imported trees and shrubs. Three quarters of a century later, this white sandstone house would become the Mineral Point Historical Museum.

During the years following the Civil War, High Street, the main street of Mineral Point, was improved with substantial business buildings of sandstone or limestone, thereby giving the city its unusual and individual style of architecture.

The first telegraph company served Mineral Point from 1849 to 1853, but failed and the line was abandoned. In 1868, a permanent telegraph line was constructed, which later was owned and operated by the Western Union Telegraph Company. [1] It served Mineral Point for three quarters of a century, then closed for lack of business.

The year 1870 is significant in the history of Mineral Point because the decennial census taken that year showed that Mineral Point had a population of 3,275, the highest in its history.

On March 17, 1874, the Graceland Cemetery Association was organized with forty charter members. This was brought about through the cooperation of all the Protestant Churches in the city. On May 24, 1875, Graceland bought a beautiful plot of land for $1,500. It lies not quite a mile from the business center of the city and has been constantly improved.

Mineral Point increasingly became the service point for the surrounding mining and agricultural region. In 1875, when the price of gold in the United States was $1.15 per ounce, the local markets in Mineral Point were considered good:

Wheat	$ .75 per bushel.
Corn	.60 per bushel.
Potatoes	.60 per bushel.
Onions	1.00 per bushel.
Butter	.18 per pound.
Eggs	.10 per dozen.

On May 23, 1878, a tornado came through the Castle Rock ravine immediately west of the city, twisted about, battered a corner of the Spensley lead smelting furnace, danced across the northern edge of the city. It unroofed houses, crumpled barns, and killed cattle. Two people in Mineral Point lost their lives and property damages were estimated at more than $30,000. [2]

One of the most prominent citizens of Mineral Point during the middle years was William A. Jones. He had been born in Wales, migrated at the age of seven with his parents to Iowa County. He was graduated from Platteville Normal School, taught school for several years, was superintendent of schools for Iowa County from 1877 to 1882, was one of the organizers of the First National Bank of Mineral Point in 1884. He was a Republican, mayor of Mineral Point and later a state assemblyman. In 1897 President McKinley appointed Jones as United States Commissioner of Indian Affairs and he served in that capacity until 1905. His part in the history of the Mineral Point Zinc Company and the Mineral Point and Northern Railroad Company will be told in the next chapter. William A. Jones erected a large and imposing home at Mineral Point which still stands and though seldom occupied, is always beautifully maintained by his surviving daughters.

In August, 1880, the County Clerk compiled a statement summarizing the principal farm products grown in Iowa County during the previous year and interestingly enough the figures were given separately for the City of Mineral Point as follows:

Wheat	700 bushels.
Corn	450 bushels.
Oats	200 bushels.
Potatoes	200 bushels.
Apples	150 bushels.

The figures for the nearby Town of Mineral Point showed that agriculture had specialized towards the production of corn, oats and wheat, and to a lesser extent to potatoes, barley, apples and rye.

In 1891, William A. Jones and his two brothers constructed an electric plant at Mineral Point. In 1906, all night electric service was begun. In 1907, the Jones brothers sold the electric plant to F. C. Ludden, who changed its name from the Mineral Point Electric Light Company to the Mineral Point Public Service Company. In 1909, Ludden expanded the business and built a transmission line to Linden, seven miles to the north. Subsequently Ludden sold the company to the Wisconsin Power and Light Company.

In the late 1890's and early 1900's, Mineral Point added a new ethnic element with an influx of immigrants from central Italy. Towards the turn of the century a group of young men from the villages of Spadule, Brugnaturi, and Zambaric in the province of Attazard emigrated to America and settled in Mineral Point. They found permanent employment in the zinc works and in the adjoining sulphuric acid plant. They had steady work and good pay and soon arranged to bring their sisters and sweethearts to Mineral Point. The men married, had large families, settled on the hill on the south side of town overlooking the zinc plant. The Italian colony brought its customs and food specialties from the old world. Each Italian family had an outdoor oven for baking bread. A fire was built in an igloo-shaped oven, and when the oven was hot, the fire was pulled out. A cloth on a stick was dipped in clear water and the inside of the oven washed clean. Sample pieces of dough were placed in the oven to test its heat and when the oven reached the correct temperature, the loaves of bread were inserted and the oven door closed. No pans were used; the loaves of bread were round and flat — and delicious, especially with red wine. The Italian people in Mineral Point paid for their homes, bought adjoining lots, planted large gardens, kept cows, chickens, pigs and even goats. During times of economic panic and depression, the Italian-American families in Mineral Point were especially resourceful and self-supporting. In time there were about 125 Italians, or Americans of Italian Descent, in Mineral Point, all regarded with ever increasing respect and affection by the older ethnic elements in the community. [3]

The burglarizing of the First National Bank of Mineral Point occurred in May, 1900. That bank was then located in a modest one story building on the north side of High Street, west of the old Court House. The facts were eventually verified by a confession signed by the lone burglar. A 26 year old man named Stewart Jelleff, alias H. C. Winter, of Ripon, Wisconsin, came to Mineral Point, secured lodgings, took his meals at Terrill's Hotel, and spent five weeks laying plans to burglarize the bank. He cut a ten foot pole from a sapling, nailed on cross strips, and made a crude ladder. On the night of Thursday, May 23, 1900, Jelleff, alias Winter, took his home-made ladder to the bank, gained access to the roof, cut an 11x12 inch hole through the roof, replaced the cut section, entered the attic and hid there twenty-four hours with no food other than a little cheese. After midnight Friday, Jelleff went to work with his burglar tools on the arched top of the bank's brick vault. He removed several bricks and dropped inside the vault. There he smashed the lock of the vault door and forced it open. He next attacked the safe and blew it open with two charges of nitro-glycerine. The explosions, though muffled by grain bags and the vault itself, did considerable property damage not only in the bank but also in the adjoining law office of Spensley and McIlhon. Jelleff took $25,290, of which $21,000 was in gold weighing some eighty-seven pounds, and $4,290 was in currency. Jelleff next picked the lock on the safe of the law firm of Spensley and McIlhon and stole the $13.00 which he found there. He left the bank building the way he had entered. City Marshal Ovitz and John Kinn made an investigation. They deduced that the heavy gold could not have been carried very far and had the city searched and recovered substantially all the loot. About $8,000 in gold was found in three bags under the board side-walk on Shake Rag Street, and $13,000 was found beneath the outhouse in the rear of Terrill's Hotel. The currency was found near Jonesdale. Meanwhile Jelleff was suspected and arrested. The prosecution for the State of Wisconsin was conducted by Joseph J. Fiedler. Later Jelleff confessed, was found guilty by the court and sentenced to the state penitentiary for a term of four to ten years. [4] At the trial or hearing Phil Allen, Jr., the cashier of the bank, made a strong plea for mercy and clemency.

Allen was the very same man who had for several years been systematically embezzling funds from the bank through an almost incredible system of false book entries, forgeries and outright thefts, all of which had been concealed from the national bank examiners during repeated examinations.

In 1907 The First National Bank of Mineral Point completed a fine new building on the south side of High Street near the main intersection. Only two years later, on Monday, October 11, 1909, the bank suddenly closed its doors. This was a story of sixteen years of criminal acts by Phil Allen, Jr. Born and reared in Mineral Point, Allen had long been a leader in business, social, and religious affairs. He was well liked, highly respected, and trusted. He had been one of the most loyal backers of Mineral Point's business ventures. He had served as president of the Mineral Point Woolen Mills and the Mineral Point Linen Fiber Company. He had helped organize the Badger Rubber Works and had become its president. He had invested in zinc mining. Not satisfied by his local interests, Allen plunged into speculative enterprises that stretched from Maine to California, most of them financed with bank funds. By 1909, he owned 2,108,370 shares of stock in 107 highly speculative enterprises, including fiber, rubber, and textile works, copper, silver, gold, and zinc mines, and telephone and electric light companies.

In October, 1909, rumors began to circulate that a shortage had been found in First National Bank funds. The people refused to believe the stories; indeed, until the day the bank went into receivership, their faith in it remained unshaken. Business continued as usual, there was no bank run, and although a few customers withdrew about $16,000, others deposited as much or more. The suspicion that something was wrong with the bank's accounts was first aroused when a bank examiner noticed that erasures and alterations had been made in the certificate of deposit register; the figure 1 had been erased to make $1300 read $300 and the figure 6 had been altered to make $6100 read $1100. Then it was discovered that there were discrepancies between the certificate register and the general ledger balance. Allen was confronted with the evidence, and although at first he denied all knowledge of the matter, he finally admitted altering the records. A detailed investigation followed, and the story of forgery, falsification of books and reports, abstraction, larceny, and embezzlement by Allen was fully disclosed. Allen's total thefts from the bank amounted to some $400,000. Beside falsifying records, forging notes, and embezzling bank funds, he sold fictitious notes to customers, took the contents of the bank vault, and stole from estates which he administered. He concealed his financial manipulations from the bank examiners, the board of directors, and his daily associates by a complicated system of accounting designed by him to make it difficult to trace entries through the books.

During the week after the bank was closed, Mineral Point was dazed. On the ensuing Sunday the city was horrified when it was discovered that Allen's brother-in-law, the cashier of the bank, Frank E. Hanscom, had gone to his father's grave in Graceland Cemetery, and after taking poison had shot and killed himself. [5] It was later found that Hanscom himself had never taken a penny, although he probably knew of Allen's nefarious schemes. [6]

The failure of The First National Bank of Mineral Point created a sensation in banking circles throughout the nation. The local, Milwaukee, and Chicago newspapers covered the story very fully. United States Comptroller Lawrence O. Murray stated that Allen "had come nearer violating every statute in his work of looting the bank than any other official of a failed bank in the history of the comptroller's office." In his book, *The Romance and Tragedy of Banking,* Thomas P. Kane, who was deputy comptroller at the time, described the bankruptcy as the "most sensational and disastrous . . . during Mr. Murray's term." Allen was described as "a genius in the art of fraud and deception." The closing of the bank left a trail of disaster in Mineral Point. Hundreds of depositors were impoverished; widows and orphans were bereft of their legacies; businessmen who had sent drafts through the bank to pay their bills were forced to pay again.

Allen was indicted on twenty-six counts, pleaded guilty to four, and was convicted and sentenced to ten years in Leavenworth, where he worked in the prison library. Even after his trial many of his old friends, who had known and trusted him for years, found it hard to believe his guilt. According to Kane, "So great was the confidence in him of many of the old customers of the bank and his church-going friends, that some of them would not believe he was guilty of the crimes charged against him until he admitted his guilt." Allen was adjudicated a bankrupt and a trustee was appointed to liquidate his assets, which finally yielded about $60,000 for the creditors.

Beginning with the closing of the bank on October 11, 1909, and for nine dreary years thereafter the receiver of the bank, Christopher L. Williams, and the lawyers and the courts systematically and methodically unravelled the many problems, proceeded against the shareholders for their double liability, collected the assets, and pressed the claims of the bank against the estate of Phil Allen, Jr., in bankruptcy; all for the benefit of the bank's depositors and all despite their fuming and seething impatience, their bitter criticism and their constant carping.

On November 3, 1909, the Comptroller of the Currency made an assessment of 100% against the shareholders and ordered the receiver to take all necessary proceedings to enforce the individual liability of each shareholder. Pursuant thereto the receiver sued one particular shareholder in the federal court at New York and carried the case through the District Court, the United States Court of Appeals for the Second Circuit, and finally in 1916 to the United States Supreme Court itself.[7]

The directors of the bank were from the most highly respected and substantial families of the city. The receiver filed suit in the United States District

Court for Western District of Wisconsin against the directors, alleging that they should have detected Allen's dishonesty, and should not have paid dividends. The master in chancery found in favor of the directors, and concluded that no serious failure in duty was proved against any of them. The master's findings, conclusions and report were approved by the District Court. The receiver appealed to the United States Circuit Court of Appeals for the Seventh Circuit, and on November 1, 1917, eight years after the closing of the bank, Judges, Baker, Kohlsaat, and Evans handed down an opinion which completely exonerated all the directors. That court adopted the findings of the master in chancery, that the directors:

". . . did not knowingly permit any of the officers, agents, or servants of The First National Bank of Mineral Point, Wis., to violate any of the provisions of the National Bank Act (Act June 3, 1864, c. 106, 13 Stat. 99); that each, so far as his duty as a director devolved upon him, diligently and honestly administered the affairs of said bank, and that each director gave to the affairs of the bank such diligence and supervision as the situation and the nature of the business required; that they exercised ordinary care and prudence in the administration of the affairs of the bank." [8]

The next year the receiver paid a final dividend, making a total of 57% paid to the depositors.

The later middle years marked several definite changes at Mineral Point. In 1910 the city paved High Street. During the next few years the city improved the streets in the residential area with grading, paving, curbs and gutters.

After the old courthouse was demolished in 1913, the city immediately began the erection on the same site of a pretentious Bedford stone and pressed brick municipal building. It combined in one structure the city hall, the free public library and a theatre for stage plays. The building cost $54,744 completely furnished. It was dedicated on February 15, 1915, with ceremonies at which appeared several of the city's clergy, both Protestant and Catholic. Three of the local lawyers gave addresses which summarized the history of the village square and the various public buildings from the early days to 1915.

The entire west half of the new civic building was an elaborate municipal theatre. There were 703 seats in the main floor and balcony and 20 chairs in the two boxes, making a total seating capacity of 723. The theatre opened on February 9, 1915. The first night performance was *The Misleading Lady,* a comedy in three acts. Ticket prices ranged from one dollar to two dollars; the opening night was sold out; the box office took in $1,153.50. The booking agency charged $500.00 and there were other expenses. The gross profit for the first night was $590.00, before any charge for the cost of the theatre. In April, 1915, a visiting stock company presented three plays during a three-night stand. In December, 1915, the Municipal Theatre announced it had arranged to show a long list of stellar attractions, including the Jack Brooks Company, Cohan, Harris and the famed Mae Robson. In the fall of 1917 the theatre scheduled the famed Irish actor, Fiske O'Hara, in a three-act comedy. Mineral Point had a fine new theatre and was enjoying first-class entertainment. For several years there were stock company plays each fall or winter, until the silent motion pictures made it economically impossible for stage plays to continue.[9]

World War I began in the middle of the summer of 1914 and the United States entered the conflict against Imperial Germany on April 7, 1917. The history of that war belongs for the most part in world and national histories; still this local history should record the facts which have a special significance for Mineral Point.

At Mineral Point a few boys enlisted in the armed services but more were drafted. The August 2, 1917 issue of the *Mineral Point Tribune* listed the names of 193 local men who had been called to duty. Many of the boys were assigned to Battery F of the 331st Field Artillery. The army had a huge training center at Camp Grant, on the outskirts of Rockford, Illinois. The Mineral Point men went by railroad to Janesville, where they changed trains and went on to Rockford and Camp Grant. After their training they were shipped overseas to France.

On the home front the people unanimously supported the war with participation in Liberty Bond Drives, doing without food needed by the armed services, wearing ersatz clothing, supporting the Red Cross and other agencies. The most significant development of the war effort at Mineral Point was the shortage of men to work at the Zinc Company. This problem was partly solved by the high school boys, who worked Saturdays, Sundays and even holidays to keep the plant in full operation for the war effort.

The tragedy of battle came home during the second year of the war. On October 4, 1918, Corporal

Lee Parkinson was wounded in the Argonne offensive in northern France; he died the same day in an ambulance while being taken to a field hospital. Only two weeks later his brother, Sergeant Homer Parkinson, of the same division was killed in action at Bantherville Forest in the Argonne offensive when he was struck by an exploding shell. The armistice occurred less than a month later.

On November 11, 1918, the central powers signed terms of surrender, an armistice was declared, and World War I was over. At Mineral Point the bells rang, the schools closed, and the people were delirious with excitement and joy. High Street turned into a carnival. Late that afternoon an orchestra was seated in the middle of High Street in front of the Municipal Building and dancing and gayety commenced and was continued into the night.

The soldiers and sailors did not return to Mineral Point until February, 1919. They were met at the railroad depot by the Mineral Point band and a large concourse of people.

As to the Parkinson brothers, their tragic loss moved the community deeply. There were impressive memorial services in May, 1919, at the Willow Springs Church, a few miles south of Mineral Point. The attendance was about 1,000. The remains were reburied in Graceland Cemetery in August, 1921. The funeral procession was the longest ever witnessed at Mineral Point and 130 World War I veterans attended. A number of Civil War Veterans also attended the burial rites in Graceland Cemetery.

The other casualties of Mineral Point men were Frank Aide, Robert Kail, Fred Padon, Samuel Jelliffe, James Brown, Thomas Phillips, Edward Schaaf, and Michael Zigersky.

An American Legion Post was organized at Mineral Point on December 31, 1919, and was named after Homer and Lee Parkinson.[10]

The further history of the middle years centers around the Mineral Point Zinc Company and the Mineral Point and Northern Railroad. That story will be told in the chapter which follows.

NOTES

[1] *History of Iowa County, Wisconsin* (Chicago, 1881), p. 692.

[2] *Ibid.*, pp. 567-572 *passim.*

[3] Pamphlet collection of Robert M. Neal, Pendarvis, Mineral Point. Italians in Mineral Point.

[4] *Mineral Point Tribune,* July 18, 1901.

[5] Report of Master in Chancery, *Williams* v. *Spensley, et al.,* U. S. D. C. W. D. Wis., Civil Docket No. 56a.

[6] *Ibid.,* p. 15.

[7] *Williams, receiver,* v. *Cobb* (1914), 2nd Cir., 219 Fed. 663. Affirmed (1916) 242 U. S. 307; 61 L. ed. 325.

[8] *Williams, receiver* v. *Spensley et al.* (1917), 7th Cir., 251 Fed. 58.

[9] *Iowa County Democrat,* Centennial Edition, Oct. 9, 1947, Section 5.

[10] *Ibid.*

XIII.

The Mineral Point Zinc Company

The Mineral Point and Northern

Railroad Company

THE EARLY LEAD MINERS discarded and threw aside as burdensome and worthless a light weight yellow substance which they called "dry-bone," because it resembled partially decayed bones. They found it in the shallow lead diggings; it appeared more plentiful as the lead mines went deeper; it became so plentiful and was considered so worthless that it was used to surface Mineral Point streets. Actually the dry bone was zinc carbonate, also called smithsonite, and it contained 52% metallic zinc.[1]

Two German scientists, Frederick W. Mathiessen and Edward C. Hegeler, who came to the United States in 1857 and arrived in Wisconsin in 1858, became the fathers of the zinc industry at Mineral Point. They toured the lead mining district, saw great piles of discarded zinc carbonate beside abandoned lead mines and heard everywhere the story of how as the lead mines were worked down to the water level, zinc ore grew more and more abundant until in the depths it appeared in greater quantities than lead. This region, they realized, was a zinc smelter's paradise. Mathiessen and Hegeler contracted to buy large quantities of the zinc carbonate. They needed coal; they went south to LaSalle, Illinois, built a furnace over the mouth of a coal mine, and shipped the zinc ore to the coal furnace for smelting. Mineral Point, formerly the capital of the lead region, would soon become the center of the zinc mines.

In 1860, Robert George and T. J. Campbell erected a small zinc furnace at Mineral Point. In 1864, they sold out Phelps, Dodge & Company, which proceeded with large-scale improvements. Thereafter the dry bone was loaded on wagons and hauled to the zinc furnace at Mineral Point, where it was smelted, or shipped by rail to LaSalle for smelting. During the years of the Civil War, the price of zinc rose to $15 a ton. The miners worked the refuse piles besides the old lead mines, and some enterprising men actually gathered up the dry bone that had been used to surface the streets. In 1869, Phelps, Dodge and Company closed its zinc works in Mineral Point and moved to Illinois, where coal was abundant and cheap.

In 1870, the output of zinc was almost equal to lead. Shortly afterwards zinc production was far greater than lead and eventually the mining industry of the Mineral Point area was mostly zinc, with lead a by-product. Most of the newer discoveries of zinc were found a few miles north of Mineral Point near the villages of Linden and Highland.

In 1882, local people organized the Mineral Point Zinc Company with a capitalization of $35,000. Mineral Point soon had a zinc oxide plant, where the zinc carbonate was converted into white zinc oxide, the basic ingredient of good paint. In 1883, three brothers, William A. Jones, David B. Jones and Thomas D. Jones, bought the Mineral Point Zinc Company, increased its capital to $400,000, and gave the business sound effective management. By 1891, the Mineral Point Zinc Company had the largest zinc oxide works in the United States. That success caused a local boom which, however, was temporarily interrupted by the nation-wide panic of 1893.[2] The Jones brothers merged their Mineral Point Zinc Company into the New Jersey Zinc Company in 1897, and that resulted in an expansion of the zinc oxide plant and the addition of a sulphuric acid plant. The entire works were located along the railroad track running south from Mineral Point, with the oxide furnace east of the track and the sulphuric acid plant to the west. The zinc industry continued to grow, and by 1900 Mineral Point was once again a booming mining and smelting town. In 1904 a rise in the price of zinc caused a large increase in the number of mines opened and in the installation of mills, separators and roasters. Minerals, this time mostly zinc ores, were once again being brought into Mineral Point in large quantities.[3]

The dry bone or zinc carbonate was gradually being exhausted and the miners turned to "black jack." That was also known as sphalerite, or zince blende, or zinc sulphide. When pure it contained 67% of metallic zinc. It was found in deep mines in the area that extended twenty miles to the north of Mineral Point. A local railroad to run from Mineral Point to the zinc mines became a necessity. For almost thirty years there had been talk of such a railroad. The idea was welcomed by the mining people of Linden and Highland, also by the farmers in that area.

In 1899 the Mineral Point and Northern Railway Company was incorporated to construct a line from Mineral Point (population 2,991) to Linden (population 543) and to Highland (population 913). Some grading was done, but by 1903 the project was at a standstill. The venture was then promoted by Charles W. McIlhon, William A. Amberg and Donald Morrill. McIlhon was born in Mineral Point, was a successful and respected local lawyer, and afterwards County Judge. Amberg had been reared at Mineral Point, but had moved to Chicago. McIlhon and Amberg were brothers-in-law. Morrill was a lawyer of high reputation and was later one of the Justices of the Appellate Court of Illinois.[4]

The first plan proposed a direct route from Mineral Point northwesterly to Linden and Highland, but that route was soon estimated to be too expensive on account of the steep hills and valleys immediately beyond the Mineral Point city limits. In consequence an alternate route was planned and carried through to completion. It used the existing tracks of the Chicago, Milwaukee and St. Paul for four miles to the south, then jackknifed back to the north and west to Linden and Highland. There were 4⅕ miles of trackage rights, plus 26⅖ miles of track owned by the Mineral Point and Northern Railway itself, a total line of 30⅗ miles. The line from Mineral Point to Highland, snaking its way through the valleys, was twice the distance as the crow flies. It crossed fourteen bridges.

The work of surveying, purchasing rights of way, and condemnation proceedings began in the spring of 1904. By June of that year, excavators, graders and pile drivers were at work. About a hundred and fifty horses and mules were employed. However, by the middle of June, 1904, the general contractor found himself in financial difficulty, whereupon the Mineral Point Zinc Company took over, gained control, and made William A. Jones superintendent and general manager. Charles W. McIlhon remained as president.[5]

In September 1904, the Mineral Point Zinc Company caused its railroad subsidiary to refund the money that had been subscribed by local citizens and the railroad was completed without local aid. That was and is a tribute to the Jones brothers, their zinc company and now their railroad. In December 1904, the laying of track was completed. All told, the railroad and equipment cost $850,000. Scheduled service began on January 1, 1905, with one round trip each day, doubled in November, 1905, to two round trips each day.

The new railroad made it possible to mine, crush, separate, concentrate and transport to the Mineral Point Zinc Company the product of the zinc mines, even low content "black jack" ore. Mineral Point and its neighboring communities to the north entered upon a new period of prosperity. By 1908, sixty-five zinc concentration mills operated in the zinc area. From Mineral Point to the end of the line at Highland, the new railroad served the flourishing zinc mines; the Peacock, the Slack, the Grunow, the Lucky Six, the Ross, the Darkhorse, the Gilman, the Rajah, the

Weigle, the Hinkle, the Optimo, the Franklin, the Wallace, the Clarke, and many more lesser zinc mines.[6] All the zinc mines were very deep and were owned by large scale operators.

In the first year of its operation, the railroad's revenues were $29,000. The expenses were $33,000 plus $14,000 interest on its bonds, a total of $47,000. Thus the loss was $18,000. The losses continued year after year and fell heavily on The Mineral Point Zinc Company as the sole bond-holder and on Mr. McIlhon, Mr. Amberg, and Mr. Morrill as the shareholders. On February 5, 1909, the Mineral Point and Northern had a wreck with a Chicago and Northwestern freight train at Whitson Junction. One man was killed and extensive property damages occurred. Another major wreck occurred on February 16, 1911, half a mile east of Highland Junction, when a train went through a bridge over the East Pecatonica River and Fireman Wald was killed. The two wrecks worsened the financial condition of the Mineral Point and Northern Railroad Company. In order to save money, service was cut to one round trip each day. Even then over a period of seven years, the railroad lost $125,000.[7]

After eight years of operation and on September 2, 1912, the Post Office withdrew its mail contract from the railroad and reintroduced horse-drawn stage coaches to haul the mail, and the city of Highland was back to horses and stage coaches.

By law, every shipper has the right to specify the routing for his shipment. When two or more lines are used, the different railroads divide the revenues, but not necessarily on a mileage basis. The Mineral

Point and Northern Railroad was able to negotiate arrangements with connecting lines whereby the Mineral Point Railroad received one-third of the freight originating or ending on its line. The other line or lines would receive the other two-thirds. For example, on a shipment from St. Paul, Minnesota, to Highland, Wisconsin, the Northwestern would bring a car 339 miles to Whitson Junction and the Mineral Point and Northern would take the car the last 8.4 miles to Highland. The total freight charge would be divided two-thirds to the Northwestern and one-third to the Mineral Point and Northern. An even more dramatic example occurred on freight shipments into Mineral Point, when the Chicago, Milwaukee and St. Paul and the Mineral Point and Northern divided the revenues two-thirds and one-third respectively, even though such shipments came the last 4.2 miles on the Milwaukee road's own tracks. The Mineral Point Zinc Company and many local merchants invariably specified shipment via the Mineral Point and Northern; nonetheless the little railroad line went further and further in the red. The Mineral Point Zinc Company came to the rescue, particularly after World War I began; and caused the railroad company to replace ties, reinforce some bridges, purchase two locomotives for $25,000 each, and add a passenger train.[8]

In 1916 the zinc mines were booming and the wages of the miners were considered very high. Wages, per day, were as follows: Crusher feeders, $2.50; Shovelers, $3.00; Hoistmen, $3.50; and Underground drill men, $5.00.

The zinc mining industry reached its peak in 1917, then declined rapidly. World War I ended with the armistice on November 11, 1918, and in 1919, the passenger train of the Mineral Point and Northern was dropped and passengers had to ride in mixed trains of freight cars and one passenger car. Late in 1920 a severe depression hit the zinc industry, the price of zinc collapsed, and the impact fell the hardest on the railroad. Its finances worsened steadily. By 1926, the Mineral Point Zinc Company owned all the $450,000 bonds issued by the railroad, plus 5,326 shares of its common stock. Mrs. Kate Amberg McIlhon, the widow of the former president of the line, and the sister of William A. Amberg owned the remaining 350 shares.[9] The Mineral Point Zinc Company offer to buy out Mrs. McIlhon and she accepted.[10] The Zinc Company became the full owner.

A series of depressing changes began to occur in Southwestern Wisconsin. The zinc mines closed one by one. The New Jersey Zinc Company, the Mineral Point division, closed the last of its zinc mines along the railroad's right of way by 1924. As the mines closed the population of Mineral Point, Linden, and Highland slowly declined. The number of passengers carried declined from 1,816 in 1924, to only 334 in 1928, less than one per day. Passenger revenues fell from $1,290 in 1924, to only $205 in 1928, or about $.55 per day. In the three winter months in 1929-

1930, the line carried only 28 passengers, or about one passenger every third day.

On January 1, 1928, the Mineral Point Zinc Company, a division of the New Jersey Zinc Company, closed all its mines in the Mineral Point area. The sulphuric acid plant operated for two months on its stockpile. A few months later the sulphuric acid plant was dismantled. With the closing of the zinc mines and the acid plant, the little railroad was doomed. Its freight revenues decreased steadily. The amount spent for repairs and maintenance likewise decreased. The line was in such poor shape that the maximum speed allowed was reduced to 20 miles per hour, with only 10 miles per hour allowed on the curves. The railroad was offered for sale to the Chicago and Northwestern and later to the Chicago, Milwaukee and St. Paul, at a price of $100,000, but neither was interested. On September 7, 1929, at the threshold of the great panic and the deep economic depression, the Mineral Point and Northern filed a petition to cease all operations. A hearing was held at Mineral Point on November 14, 1929; the Railroad Commission entered a ruling on January 1, 1930, permitting abandonment; the physical assets were sold for scrap for less than $50,000, and all purchasers removed their property by the end of 1930.

After 26 years of operation, the right-of-way became a strip of neglected land, with wild flowers and wild grape vines gradually covering the scars.[11]

A few zinc mines at Mineral Point and to the west of Mineral Point remained open and shipped their ores by truck. Several new mines opened during World

War II. As this book is written the mines still in operation are very deep and produce about 90% zinc concentrate and 10% lead concentrate.

NOTES

[1] *History and Guide to Mineral Point* (W. P. A. Federal Writers' Project, *Circa* 1941, State Historical Society of Wisconsin, Madison), pp. 216, 217.

[2] Wisconsin Magazine of History, Vol. 38, p. 4.

[3] *Ibid.*, pp. 4, 5.

[4] *Ibid.*, pp. 6, 47. Morrill was later a Judge of the Appellate Court of Illinois at Chicago.

[5] *Ibid.*, p. 48.

[6] *Ibid.*, p. 95.

[7] *Ibid.*, p. 96.

[8] *Ibid.*, pp. 96-98 *passim.*

[9] *Ibid.*, p. 100.

[10] Interviews of author with Kate Amberg McIlhon.

[11] Wisconsin Magazine of History, Vol. 38, pp. 102-105, *passim.*

XIV.

The Centennial in 1927

The Years of the Depression

AFTER ONE hundred years, the city was becoming increasingly conscious of its historical heritage and in 1927 Mineral Point celebrated its Centennial. This occasion was probably the largest and most successful community-sponsored event ever held in the town. The celebration was held on August 2nd, 3rd, 4th and 5th. Historical places were marked: the Jerusalem Spring, the Methodist Church, the site of Fort Jackson, St. Paul's Mission Church, Trinity Church, the site of the United States Land Office and others. The stores up and down High Street displayed relics from the past; there was a parade of fifty floats, each depicting some event in the long history of Mineral Point. The Centennial was widely promoted: there were more than five hundred homecomers who registered from places all the way from New York to California and from Maine to Texas. It was estimated that there were five thousand people each day at Mineral Point during the celebration. There was a Pageant of Progress at the Fair Grounds with three hundred local people in the cast, depicting one hundred years of history: the Indians, the discovery of the lead mines, the Black

Hawk War in 1832, the inauguration of Gov. Dodge on July 4, 1836, the Gold Rush in 1849, the cholera in 1850, the Civil War from 1861 to 1865, the Great War from 1914 to 1917, the completion of the new high school in 1925.[1]

On August 18, 1928 Mineral Point dedicated the site of Old Fort Defiance, four miles south of the city, for its part in shielding the city from roving bands of Indians during the Black Hawk War. Governor Fred R. Zimmerman came from Madison and delivered an address for the dedication.

The years 1927 and 1928 not only marked one hundred years of history, but coincidentally marked the end of an era of progress and the beginning of the great depression which would continue for ten or twelve long and grinding years. It should be understood that the depression actually began in Mineral Point in 1927 and 1928 when the decisions were made to close the zinc mines, the Mineral Point Zinc Works and the Mineral Point and Northern Railroad. At that time no one dreamed of the depth and duration of the hard times to come. Two years later in the fall of 1929 an economic panic hit the entire country and the grim economic depression was then upon Mineral Point with all its cruel consequences.

From 1929 to 1932 the economic life in Mineral Point was alternately in panic and at a standstill. There had been two banks, The Iowa County Bank and The Farmers and Citizens Bank, which in 1931 merged under the name of The Consolidated Bank of Mineral Point in order to gain strength through union. How-

156

ever, both banks were weak and early in 1932 the consolidated institution was in financial trouble. During the first seven months of 1932 public meetings were held, voluntary waivers were solicited, public support was urged to keep the bank doors open. All to no avail. The bank was closed permanently in July, 1932; the state banking department proceeded with liquidation; Mineral Point was virtually paralyzed. This was the third bank failure in Mineral Point: [2]

The Bank of Mineral Point, closed in 1841.

The First National Bank of Mineral Point, closed in 1909.

The Consolidated Bank of Mineral Point, closed in 1932.

The inhabitants of Mineral Point, like many people at all times in all places, had wanted banks which would be ready and willing to accommodate easily with loans but at the same time would be sound and strong. Such opposite desires and illogical thinking contributed at least in part to the three bank failures in a century of banking at Mineral Point.

After three years of inconvenient, clumsy and threadbare life without a local bank, the Farmers Savings Bank at nearby Edmund established its main banking quarters at Mineral Point. In April, 1935 the bank opened at Mineral Point with resources totaling only $280,000. One year later the resources of this bank had increased to $656,000, a remarkable growth considering the hard times. This institution proceeded to give the citizens the great benefits that flow from a sound, strong, strict, disciplined and well-managed bank. More than anything else this bank kept alive the economic and business life of Mineral Point during the bleak days of the depression.

The 1930's saw Mineral Point with a static population, declining property values, many of the houses occupied by families which had to receive public assistance. An old town becoming more shabby with each passing season and year. Many of the farms in the surrounding countryside had been heavily mortgaged in favor of insurance companies, which either proceeded with foreclosure or took quitclaim deeds from the farmers in satisfaction of the mortgage debt. A drive by automobile in any direction would disclose the repossessed farms, which when taken over by an insurance company would be repaired and improved and would have the farmhouse painted white and the barn red. During the second half of the decade the insurance companies went forward with plans for the sale of these farms and many sales were made to the same people who had formerly owned the same land.

At Mineral Point, as elsewhere, the most cruel consequence of the depression was increasing unemployment. In order to relieve that condition, the United States government sponsored several public works projects for the town. One was a writer's project, which produced the "History and Guide to Mineral Point." The work was typewritten and bound in book form but never printed.[3] Another project was the construction in 1936-1937 of the municipal swimming pool. It was built with local limestone and cost about $35,000, most of the funds having gone into labor. It was opened July 15, 1937.

Mineral Point had for more than one hundred years assumed that the roads leading into the city would be more or less closed during the most severe weeks of the winter months. For several years the people of Mineral Point had urged that the road to Dodgeville should be straightened, levelled, and paved with concrete. Those plans were realized in 1937 and in August of that year the concrete road was completed and opened with ribbon-cutting ceremonies.[4]

As the depression ground on and on for some twelve years at Mineral Point, its citizens saw ever more clearly the consequences of the loss of the county seat. For it was true that during the seventy-five years from the loss of the county seat in 1861 to the bottom of the depression in 1936, Mineral Point had remained ahead of Dodgeville in many ways. However, during the depression big government spending began and filtered the money through the county seat towns, much to their relative advantage. Mineral Point began to lose out to its ancient rival, Dodgeville, in population and in prosperity.

The depression brought out and developed with clarity that Mineral Point was no longer a lead and zinc mining town. To be sure, there were a few deep mines still operating in the area and now and then promoters would drill to locate or to prove the existence of new ore bodies. The shift was to agriculture, mainly cattle raising and dairying. The shift from the psychology of mining to the psychology of farming produced many subtle changes, not only in Mineral Point but in all of southwestern Wisconsin. The main difference was the end of dreams of riches that could come from striking a lead or zinc mine. In the future at Mineral Point economic success would come only through hard work on the farms or in the service trades, and through thrift.

By 1939, when World War II began in Europe, Mineral Point was emerging from the great depression. It was, for the most part, an unpainted, shabby old town with many shacks, shanties and outdoor privies. It remained that way even through the war years to 1945.

NOTES

[1] Centennial Program, 1827-1927.

[2] *Iowa County Democrat* and *Mineral Point Tribune*. October 8, 1947. Section 5, p. 3.

[3] *History and Guide to Mineral Point* (W. P. A. Federal Writers' Project, State Historical Society of Wisconsin.)

[4] *Iowa County Democrat* and *Mineral Point Tribune*. October 9, 1847.

XV.

The Cornish and Mineral Point

THE DUCHY of Cornwall is the most southern and western part of Great Britain. It is the mountainous rock rib that extends out to Land's End, and is surrounded by the sea on all sides but one. Cornwall is a mining region, more especially a tin mining country. It is poor and sparsely settled. In numbers the Cornish have always been few; only 300,000 even in modern times. There is no large city in Cornwall.

The Cornish are Celts. During the fifth century the Teutonic Angles and Saxons invaded Britain and drove the resident Celts west and south into the fastness of Cornwall. It took four centuries to subdue the Cornish; next followed more than a thousand years of rule by the English. But Cornwall stood apart from the general life of England, cut off by differences in blood and speech and feudal tendencies. The Cornish clung to local chieftains with Celtic loyalty. They retained many marks of their Celtic civilization. They have consistently considered and referred to themselves as Cornishmen, not Englishmen.

The Phoenicians, the Romans, the Moors, and the Spanish sailed their trading ships to Cornwall, where they secured tin from the Cornish miners. The Spanish traded saffron for tin.

The men of Cornwall have, through the many centuries, been famous as miners and were reputed to be the best tin miners and hard rock miners in the world. They were expert with the pick and gad and had an almost uncanny ability in angles, elevations, inclines and directions underground.

After the turn of the century in 1800, the Cornish tin mines were either exhausted or too deep to work profitably. Thousands of miners were gradually thrown out of work and had to look elsewhere. Many went overseas and a few went to America.[1]

The previous pages of this book have outlined the working of the lead mines in the upper Mississippi Valley successively by the French, the Indians, the southerners who migrated back and forth like "suckers," and the Yankees who came and stayed and lived in dugouts like "badgers."

The first Cornishman to come to the lead region was Francis Clyma, who emigrated to America in 1819, engaged in mining in Maryland, Virginia, Kentucky and Missouri. He went to Galena in March, 1827, and after a few weeks prospecting struck lead near Gratiot's Grove, which lies a mile south of present day Shullsburg and twenty miles south of Mineral Point. Francis Clyma had heard of these rich mines after he had been in the United States for some time. There is no record of any other Cornishmen coming to the lead mines until 1830, when there began a stream of direct emigration from Cornwall that lasted more than twenty years.[2] Most of the Cornish who came to the lead region immigrated from the vicinity of Camborn, a little city of 8,000. They embarked on sailing vessels from the ports of Penzance and Falmouth on the southern coast of Cornwall, crossed the sea in sailing vessels in six weeks, ascended the Missisippi to Galena and walked on to Mineral Point and its vicinity.

As the Cornish miners, some with their families, arrived at Mineral Point in the early 1830's, they settled as squatters on both sides of the lane at the foot of the hill and that locality became known as Shake Rag Under The Hill.

The early Cornish immigrant miners had little or no schooling. About three-fourths of them could neither read nor write. They were characteristically honest, hard working, thrifty and deeply religious in their staunch Methodist faith. They were not addicted to hard liquor but enjoyed a glass of beer. When the Cornish miner first arrived, he usually began to work as a laborer at fifteen or twenty dollars per month with room and board. He much preferred to prospect and mine for himself, however, and not be employed by others.

The early lead miners of other ethnic groups dug ore from surface outcroppings. They also dug float mineral between the surface of the earth and the beginning of solid rock. They did only a little blasting because they used merely an inefficient row of straws as a fuse to the charge of blasting powder. The early miners always abandoned their diggings when they struck solid rock. This was the unique opportunity for the Cornish miners. They brought with them their ancient skills as hard rock miners plus the safety fuse which had been invented in Cornwall by a man named Davis. It was a small white cord filled with combustible material inserted during the process of manufacture. It was a simple invention but it worked well and it gave sufficient time to the miner to get out of the mine or retreat behind an angle in a tunnel before the spark touched the blasting powder and set off the explosion with its shower of rock.[3]

The Cornish miners went to the abandoned lead diggings and dug through rock, soft and hard. They blasted shafts, tunnels and drifts. They extracted hundreds of millions of pounds of lead ore. As a boy this author, carrying a home made paraffin candle, walked through many miles of abandoned tunnels and drifts, always marveling at the skill exhibited by the Cornish lead miner.

There are no precise statistics on the number of Cornish who emigrated from Cornwall to the lead region. The best authority is Copeland who said: "The Cornish at no period exceeded in number a fifth of the total population of the district. Should we estimate their number in 1850 at that ratio, there would be about 7,000 of them, and there were more Cornish immigrants in the lead region then, than before or since. It was just before the rush to California set in, which took away so many of Wisconsin's Cornish miners. To arrive at a closer estimate of the number of Cornish immigrants, let us examine the following (1850) census reports of the principal Cornish settlements, and make an estimate of the proportion of Cornishmen to the entire population:" [4]

	Population	Probably Cornish
Mineral Point	2,110	1,100
Dodgeville	2,580	1,300
Hazel Green	1,840	950
Linden	950	750
Shullsburg	1,600	400
		4,500

Copeland goes on and adds the Cornish in other mining settlements to reach the total Cornish immigration to the upper Mississippi lead region at the aforesaid 7,000. After 1850 the proportion of Cornish in Mineral Point declined as the Cornish moved to the gold mines and as immigrants from other countries arrived; so that by 1890 the Cornish formed only about one third of the population of Mineral Point.

The Cornish were also skilled stone cutters and masons. The hillsides on either side of Shake Rag Street were opened here and there as quarries for building stone. The limestone, as it was quarried, was damp, easily cut, shaped, squared, dressed and drilled. The early Cornish used the limestone at hand and built about 30 houses along Shake Rag Street. Some of these were only a dozen feet in front of the quarry from which the stone had been taken.

In 1910, the stone houses were then only 75 years old, were in fair condition, were all occupied and were given at least some care and maintenance. However, these houses had never been modernized, had no running water, no indoor plumbing, no central heat, and only a few were wired for electricity. When the zinc mines became exhausted and the Mineral Point Railroad was discontinued and the great zinc furnace was closed, Mineral Point went into a serious economic and social decline. Mute testimonies were the old Cornish miners' houses, many of which became unoccupied and began to fall into ruin.

At the bottom of the depression in 1935, a former local boy who had been employed in the Chicago, New York, and London antique shops of the famed Mrs. Somerset Maugham, left London, returned to Mineral Point and became deeply interested in Cornish lore and the Cornish houses on Shake Rag Street. He began a Cornish restoration a full century after the first arrival here of Cornishmen. He was Robert M. Neal, himself of Cornish descent. He and an associate, Edgar Hellum, bought the one story stone cottage, now known as Pendarvis House. Its walls were eighteen inches thick, solid limestone, cut from the small quarry opened in the hillside a few feet in the rear. The front of the little house had stones that were cut, dressed, and faced. The stone work in the front wall was so fine that the limestone blocks fit almost perfectly and required little mortar to be set. The side and rear walls were of uncut stones. The south wall was a ruin; the alternate freeze and thaw during a hundred Wisconsin winters had thrown the wall fourteen inches out of plumb. The sole occupant of that house, a man living like a hermit, had closed the openings at the roof line by stuffing old quilts in the open spaces.

Robert M. Neal and Edgar Hellum proceeded with a restoration. They moved slowly and carefully but worked persistently. In a few years they acquired the three story stone and log house to the south, which they called Polperro, and the two story house to the north which they called Trelawney. The three houses were so named because of the old couplet in the writings of Walter Scott, "By Tre, Pol and Pen we know the Cornishmen." Neal and Hellum also acquired several adjacent lots in which they arranged informal gardens which greatly improved the area.[5]

The team of Neal and Hellum had some professional help, particularly from Charles Curtis, an eighty-five year old stone mason, who had been born in Cornwall, and who had a deep love for all things Cornish. Gradually the little locality on old Shake Rag Street became increasingly interesting and attractive as the houses were restored and as the rock gardens and rock walls became covered with creeping green vines, moss and rock cress.

The interiors were, if possible, even more interesting and attractive. One room on the second floor of Trelawney contains Mr. Neal's collection of Wisconsiana, undoubtedly the finest privately-owned collection of books dealing with the history of the Wisconsin lead and zinc region.

As a part of the Cornish restoration at Mineral Point, the owners of Pendarvis developed a new interest in old Cornish foods.

In Cornwall the miners had for centuries gone to the mines carrying a "pasty" for their noon lunch. A pasty was almost an ideal food to carry to a mine and deserves to be described in some detail. The miner's wife would roll out pasty dough, much like a pie crust, onto which she would put cubes of beef, chopped suet, sliced potatoes, onions and rutabagas. The dough would be folded across the top and whole baked on a flat stone or pan. The miner would carry the pasty to the mine in the pocket of his jacket, or in his dinner pail, for his one dish noon meal. If the mine had a steam engine, the pasty would be placed near the steam pipes. At noon, the pasty would be warm and tasty for the miner's lunch. The Cornish miners brought this custom with them when they emigrated to the lead mines in and around Mineral Point. Cornish pasties came to be fancied not only by the miners and their families but also by other people of Mineral Point of all the many ethnic origins.

Another Cornish specialty was baked goods with saffron. First quality saffron is the dried stigma of the Spanish autumn blooming crocus, gathered when the crocus is in full bloom. It has a brilliant yellow color and a highly distinctive flavor. As this book is written, Spanish saffron retails at $96.00 a pound. The grocery stores and other shops in Mineral Point have long done a large business in saffron, considering the small size of the town, and now almost every household in Mineral Point makes saffron buns and saffron cake, especially at Christmas time.

A dessert or "sweet" much enjoyed by the Cornish consists of wild gooseberries or wild plums with scalded clotted cream. Clotted cream is difficult to make. Large quantities of milk are heated slowly but without boiling; at a proper time the cream that forms and clots in the top is skimmed off.

For more than one hundred and twenty-five years Cornish pasties, saffron buns, and scalded cream have been enjoyed in all the houses and restaurants at Mineral Point. On almost every day of the week one restaurant or another will display a sign "Pasties Today." Pendarvis House, now very fashionable, prepares and serves pasties on advance reservation during the short summer season.

The Cornish in southwestern Wisconsin settled in groups only because of the lead mines. The Cornish in America were never clannish. They kept no close ties with their homeland. They founded no national societies. They never feared to unite with others in any community effort. They never hesitated to marry with other nationalities. When the mines played out they began to disperse and progressively lost their identity as an ethnic unit.

At Mineral Point the Cornish restoration and the interest in Cornish foods and customs during the 1930's, came just in time to preserve an interesting chapter in the history of the lead region.

NOTES

[1] *The Peoples of Wisconsin*, State Historical Society of Wisconsin, Madison, July, 1955, pp. 11-15, *passim*.
[2] Wisconsin Historical Collections, Vol. XIV, pp. 305, 306.
[3] *Ibid.*, pp. 319, 320.
[4] *Ibid.*, p. 312.
[5] *Wisconsin Magazine of History*, Vol. 29, pp. 391-401, *passim*.

XVI.

The Churches and the Schools

THE PREVIOUS pages of this book have mentioned the churches and the schools in the early days of Mineral Point. A more detailed history of both should now be given. Mineral Point has six churches, four of them Protestant, two Catholic. Their history will be reviewed in the order in which they were founded at Mineral Point.

The First Methodist Church

The First Methodist Church of Mineral Point is the oldest Protestant organization and congregation in the State of Wisconsin.

At Mineral Point the history of the Protestant faith goes all the way back to 1828, when Elder William Roberts, the pioneer miner-preacher, held services and led his congregation in singing "Jerusalem My Happy Home" and other stirring Christian hymns. The miners who came to see and hear Elder Roberts called him the "Great High Priest" and the spring near which he held services the "Jerusalem Spring." Many of the early miners were Methodist.

In 1834, the Methodists erected a little log church, 24 feet wide and 30 feet long, some fifteen or twenty rods from the Mansion House, a little to the left of the foot of present day High Street. It was built entirely of logs, excepting the sawed boards for the windows and doors. The next year on December 5, 1835, the Rev. Alfred Bronson, the famous pioneer Methodist circuit rider, visited Mineral Point. He wrote the following in his journal:

"Dec. 5. Rode to Mineral Point. The next day being Sabbath I preached. This town contains about 600 inhabitants, mostly miners & the place derived its name & wealth from the abundance of its mineral resources. It is unpleasantly situated, 3 miles from any amount of timber." [1]

As to the log church, Rev. Bronson described it in a letter as follows: [2]

"Dear Sir: The first Methodist Episcopal, and the first Protestant church built in Wisconsin, was erected at Mineral Point in 1834. It was of logs entirely. I think there was not a sawed board in it, except what was worked into window-sash and doors. The logs were notched together at the corners, chinked inside, and daubed or plastered outside with clay mortar. The floor was of puncheons split out of logs and smoothed with a broad-ax on the flat side, the round side being spotted to fit the sleepers. The roof was made of clapboards, split out of large oak trees, and the ceiling and pulpit were made from the same material. The seats were made of split logs smoothed on the flat side, with wooden pegs driven into auger holes for legs. I do not remember whether the door hinges were made of wood or iron. I think it was about 20 x 30 feet in area. It stood on the first spur or point of land that comes in from the northwest, some fifteen or twenty rods from Abner Nichol's old hotel, near the foot of Commerce street.

"I held the first quarterly meeting; gave the first love feast, and administered the first sacrament in it, in the fall of 1835. . . .

Respectfully,

Alfred Bronson"

In 1836, Rev. Richard Homey was appointed minister; he also taught a Protestant school for the children. The next year, in 1837, the Rev. John Crummer came to Mineral Point. By then the society had increased to 30 members. During the fall of that year a small rock church was built on a corner near the present structure.

The Rev. T. M. Fullerton arrived at Mineral Point in March, 1841. According to his testimony:

"My first sight of Iowa County was March 19, 1841. It then included all the territory now in LaFayette County. I shall confine this paper chiefly to matters pertaining to the Methodist Episcopal Church. At that time Mineral Point charge or circuit embraced Dodgeville and Peddler's Creek, now Linden; but for want of preachers, Hamilton's Grove Circuit was added that year, all under the care of Rev. James G. Whitford, whom I came to assist on the added part. Mr. Whitford lived in a small house, rented for the purpose . . .

". . . At Mineral Point, the old log church still served for a place of worship, but soon gave place to a stone chapel, which was half of the present workshop near the new church. It then, when first built, faced the town. Afterwards it was enlarged to its present size, and the roof turned north and south.

"In 1843-44, I was the Pastor at Mineral Point, including Dodgeville and Peddler's Creek. There was no parsonage. Rooms were hired for the preacher of N. Coad. The first part of the chapel above described was then finished, and was considered a very fine thing. In it, on my first Sunday, I heard for the first time instrumental music in a church, and it converted me from doubts of its propriety. It was within the altar railing, and consisted of bass viol by George Priestly, a clarinet and two flutes." [3]

In 1848, certain differences arose among the members of the Methodist Episcopal Church and there were opposing views over the purchase and use of an organ. On the first Sunday after the installation of the organ, two choirs took places in the church. One sang a cappella, the other sang accompanied by the organ. By the next Sunday, the whole congregation had taken sides and about seventy members withdrew and subsequently formed the Primitive Methodist Church of Mineral Point.[4] The original congregation continued its progress and within a few years made plans for a much larger church.

In 1857, during the pastorate of the Rev. Lawton, the subject of a new Methodist church edifice was urged, but nothing was accomplished effectively until 1867. A committee of Rev. Lawton, James Spensley and Edward Hosking was appointed and secured substantial pledges. A New York architect was retained, and in 1869 the corner stone was laid for a large new edifice. It was to be of white sandstone, to be taken from a local quarry. The work went ahead during 1869, 1870 and 1871. The sandstone was quarried, cut into blocks and taken by horse and wagon from the quarry to the jobsite. Straw was put into the wagons and placed between the stones to prevent chipping and cracking, newly quarried sandstone being soft. The structure was completed and dedicated in 1871. The cost was $32,000.[5] It stood forth as an impressive and beautifully constructed English Gothic church, with the exterior stone cut as delicately as though the masons had worked with wood. In 1904 the church purchased and installed a pipe organ at a cost of $2,000.

The Methodist Church stands at the head of High Street on the most prominent site in Mineral Point. The exterior walls are no longer soft but have weathered and hardened. The stonework of this church, done by the early Mineral Point craftsmen, will for many generations stand as a monument to the art of the stone cutter, and the church edifice will stand for many future generations as a Christian inspiration in the community.

On Sunday, January 8, 1961, the members of the First Methodist Church held a meeting and by a vote of sixty to twelve approved a long range program of modernization and improvements. The cost was estimated at $143,000.

As this history is written, in 1962, the minister is the Rev. Wesley C. Hunter.

St. Paul's Catholic Church

The first Catholic priest to visit Mineral Point was the famous pioneer missionary, Rev. Samuel Mazzuchelli, a Dominican. He had been born and educated at Milan in northern Italy; had emigrated to the United States. He had been ordained in Cincinnati; had labored at many missions in the vast northwest regions. In April, 1835, when Mineral Point was still in Michigan Territory, and in religion was in the Diocese of Detroit, Fr. Mazzuchelli, while on his travels, stopped at Mineral Point. He wrote in his own "Memoirs" that he:

". . . traveled on horseback first to a village called Mineral Point. At this place it pleased Divine Providence to grant him means most timely and necessary for continuing his long journey. A gentleman of the place desired him to baptize his three children and invited him also to preach in one of the houses. He willingly consented and this having been done, as he was remounting his horse next morning, the father of the newly baptized children put into his hand the sum of twenty dollars. 'May God be thanked!' was the only word the recipient could utter, for without his assistance he would not have been able to accomplish a tenth part of the distance yet to be traversed. The keeper of the hotel, too, although a Protestant, declined to take his just due for the traveler's entertainment." [6]

On April 9, 1835, at Mineral Point, Fr. Mazzuchelli preached a sermon on "The Works of the Catholic Church." His listeners were mostly Protestants, there being only a few Catholics at Mineral Point at that time.

Father Mazzuchelli first said Mass at Mineral Point in 1838. The service was held in a log shanty owned by Mrs. Uren and rented to James Smith, an Irish Catholic. A little later Mr. Smith moved to a residence located back of where the present municipal building stands and Catholic services were again conducted in his private home.

The congregation was organized as a mission about the year 1839. The people first rented a house owned by a Mr. Crawford. As one of his many missions, Fr. Mazzuchelli visited the congregation at irregular intervals until 1841 or 1842.

The next priest to attend the mission was the Rev. James Causse, a Frenchman. He was a priest of the Diocese of Detroit and was stationed at Potosi in Wisconsin Territory. He came to Mineral Point once a month. In 1842, through the efforts of Fr. Causse, a church of limestone and sandstone was commenced, twenty-eight feet wide and forty feet long. The congregation was made up of all nationalities and classes, but the majority at this time were Irish. They had left Ireland because of its desperate economic condition, had landed at seaports in the east and at New Orleans, and had filtered to the Wisconsin frontier to work as miners, as farmers, and at other occupations.

At this early date the members of the congregation were scattered over a territory many miles in every direction. In order to attend services, some were compelled to travel twenty-five miles or more, and to be away from their homes and their work from two to three days. Fr. James Causse continued at intervals to attend the church until 1844, or a little later.[7]

Territorial Wisconsin was constituted a separate diocese in 1843, with John Martin Henni as the first bishop. Soon thereafter, Bishop Henni gave attention to Mineral Point. Among the source material that mentions early Mineral Point are the letters of the Rev. Adelbert Inama, translated from the German and published by the Wisconsin State Historical Society. Father Inama was the pastor of the Catholic Church at Sac Prairie (*sic*). On December 12, 1845, at Sac Prairie the Reverend Father wrote on his work in the territory of Wisconsin:

"The congregation here is indeed not yet numerous, so this winter I have spare time to devote to the instruction of the school children. Next year assuredly one must count on a very large increase. The Bishop has at the same time added to my pastoral activity the care of the capital Madison, twenty-five miles distant; Mineral Point, forty-eight miles . . . ."[8]

The foregoing letter does not give the exact date when Bishop Henni assigned "pastoral activity" at Mineral Point. The sequence of dates indicates 1844 or early 1845.

Rev. Inama wrote in another of his letters about a visit he made at Mineral Point in the fall of 1845:

"At noon we arrived at the little mining town of Mineral Point, which owes its existence solely to the mines and is inhabited for the most part by miners, among them many Catholics. Their stone church is nearing completion, and lately a Frenchman was appointed as their pastor." [9]

The reference in the above letter to the "completion" of the stone church, must have been the structure commenced in 1842; and the reference to the French priest must have been to the Rev. Victor Jouanneault, who became the first resident pastor, appointed by Bishop Henni. Bishop Henni blessed the stone church on December 7, 1845. Fr. Jouanneault assumed charge on September 24, 1846.

According to the printed "The Catholic Almanac 1846" this mission congregation was then called St. Charles.[10] The later references to the parish always give the name as St. Paul's.

During the 1849-1850 cholera epidemic the members of this parish offered public prayers for the intercession of the Mother of God to be spared from the plague; and there is a well founded tradition that not a single parishioner died of the dreaded disease.

On January 21, 1851, the men of St. Paul's organized the Hibernian Temperance Association. It flourished for several years only.

Until 1851 the Catholics at Mineral Point were interred in the church lots adjoining the church and rectory. With the growth of the town and the parish and the erection of various residences in the vicinity of the church, it became a practical necessity to locate a separate and more suitable cemetery. On July 6, 1851, at a meeting of the congregation, it was decided to purchase an acre of land two or three blocks south on "The Galena Road" (now U.S. Highway 151) for a burial ground. As many of the bodies buried in the church yard as could be found were removed to the new burying ground.

The congregation increased rapidly; the original stone church became too small; in May, 1855, the cornerstone was laid for a second stone church to be forty feet wide and eighty feet long. However, on account of hard times or other difficulties, progress on the second church was slow and it was not completed and dedicated until July 29, 1860.

Beginning in the late 1850's and early 1860's the German speaking Catholic population of Mineral Point increased so rapidly that they soon numbered as many families as the Irish, and in 1870 St. Paul's congregation was divided and St. Mary's congregation was then founded.

St. Paul's second stone church served from 1860 to 1910 and was last used for divine service on April 17, 1910. It was then demolished and in 1911 the present church was completed at a cost of some $20,000. It is vitrified brick with Bedford stone trim. St. Paul's has a seating capacity of four hundred and fifty persons.[11]

The old, original stone church, now known as the Mission Church, still stands as a monument to the pioneers. It is one of the oldest church buildings still standing in sound condition in all Wisconsin. The centennial of the Mission Church was celebrated in 1942, at which time the parish published a booklet which outlined the long history of this congregation.

At this writing, the pastor of St. Paul's Congregation is Father Harry J. Lauters.

Trinity Episcopal Church

As early as 1836, Bishop Jackson Kemper conducted Episcopal services at Mineral Point. He preached here on July 26, 1838. Either he or Father Gear or the Rev. Richard F. Cadle visited Mineral Point as a mission during the three years from 1836 to 1839.

The Miner's Journal of June 11, 1839, reported: "The Rev. Mr. Weed will preach at the log court house Sunday next at ten A.M. and at three P.M. on the cornerstone of the new church."

The next year, in 1840, Moses M. Strong donated a whole block to the Episcopal congregation and money was raised to build a church. The erection of a church building was commenced in the spring of 1840 on the lot where the present edifice stands. The walls were of rough limestone and of rude construction and were only partially erected when the work was stopped and never resumed, owing to financial difficulties. The Episcopal parish became dormant for five years, during which period no formal records were kept.

In September, 1845, in territorial days, Rev. Ebenezer Williams came to Mineral Point, the congregation was revived, a vestry was organized, the parish was called Trinity Church. On October 6, 1845, it was resolved by the vestry to erect a church to cost $5,000; a committee was appointed to raise the necessary funds; another committee was appointed to see to the actual construction.[12]

In the spring of 1846, pending construction, the parish sought the use of the then new courthouse as a temporary place to hold divine services. On April 10, 1846, the Iowa County Commissioners at a meeting held at Mineral Point passed the following resolution in behalf of the parish:

"Ordered that a lease be granted on part of the Broad (sic) of County Commissioners to the Wardens and Vestery (sic) of Trinity Church Mineral Point for the use of the Court Room in the Court House on Sabbath days only for the term of six months from this date.

Which said lease is this day executed and placed on file. Terms $20.00 per annum." [13]

The work on the church went steadily ahead with substantial completion accomplished by October, 1846. The foundations were buff limestone ashlar. The walls were vermilion brick made of local clay and fired at Mineral Point; the windows and capstones on the tower were of beautifully-cut buff limestone. The tower was crenellated and housed a bell. The result was a small Gothic Revival architectural gem of singular simplicity and beauty.

In August, 1855, Bishop Kemper, assisted by the clergy of the Diocese of Wisconsin, consecrated the Trinity Episcopal Church.

The Rev. Lyman Phelps became rector in March, 1865, and during his pastorate the parish built a substantial and beautiful sandstone rectory, Gothic in style, at a cost of $6,700.

In 1865, the parish school was erected at a cost of $3,000. It was a simple one-story frame building but well lighted and ventilated. It was capable of seating 150 pupils. The minister's wife was the first teacher; she continued until her death in 1872; the school was closed in 1874.

In 1881, the Rev. March Chase became rector and continued serving the parish for thirty-two years until he retired in 1914, and moved to Winnetka, Illinois.

In 1889 Trinity Episcopal Church graciously entered into a five-year lease with the City of Mineral Point whereby the Parish Hall was used as a public primary school.

In 1934, during the great depression, the church was listed as a mission and for a time was served by the rector from Platteville or Lancaster.

After more than a century, the fabric of the edifice began to show the need for extensive repairs. The entire Episcopal Diocese, particularly the children with their mite boxes, came to the rescue, and in 1957, 1958, 1959 and 1960 extensive repairs were made, the foundations were strengthened, the entire church was beautifully restored.

The pastor at the present time, 1962, is the Rev. Canon John E. Flockhart.

The First Congregational Church

The Primitive Methodist Church was organized at Mineral Point by the Rev. Joseph Hewett early in 1848 with eighty-two members, of whom about seventy had just withdrawn from the Methodist Episcopal Church. During the first year meetings were held in various homes of the members. The next year, in 1849, an attractive buff limestone church, facing the east, was erected at a cost of $2,200. Two years later, in 1851, a gallery was built inside the church at a cost of $800. The membership of this congregation grew rapidly and the Mineral Point Primitive Methodist

Church became the headquarters of a circuit that extended forty miles east and west and at least as many miles north and south. The circuit preachers were under the supervision of three ministers stationed at Mineral Point. The pioneer stone church was razed in 1890, but parts of its lower walls were allowed to stand and can still be seen by the student of local history. A very similar stone church can be seen at the nearby village of Linden.

In place of the original church, a much larger frame structure was partially constructed in 1892 and completed in 1893. It cost $30,000. *The Mineral Point Tribune* of August, 1893, carried the story of the dedication and said: "The new church is a frame building with a stone foundation, which furnishes a magnificent room for Sunday School purposes, and other meetings, seating capacity 600. The auditorium seats 700, and a chapel capable of seating 200 is arranged as to be connected with the Auditorium. Above the chapel are three commodious class rooms." The new church was surmounted, at its northeast corner, with a tall spire, part of which was later removed. The church was originally equipped with a foot pump reed organ. A great new pipe organ was installed in 1913 at a cost of $2,000.

In 1913, the congregation voted to sever its connection with the Western Conference of the Primitive Methodist Church and to affiliate with the Congregational Conference of Wisconsin. The circumstances, with interesting sidelights on the history of Mineral Point, were set forth in the November, 1913, issue of the Congregational Church Life Magazine:

"The Mineral Point Primitive Methodist Church of two hundred members was recognized by Council, October 14th, as the First Congregational Church of Mineral Point.

"Rev. W. J. C. Bond, himself originally a Primitive Methodist minister, became a Congregationalist about eighteen years ago. While a Primitive Methodist minister he was pastor of this church for five years. After serving our church at Boscobel for twelve years as a Congregational minister, and then taking a year of rest, he returned to Mineral Point where for over five years, as a Congregational minister he has served this church. Meanwhile the church was practically independent with growing Congregational tendencies although retaining formal connection with the Primitive Methodist body.

"With the growing feeling that they needed a larger fellowship, and that they ought to have increased opportunity and responsibility for the extension of the Kingdom of God, the one hundred and ten voting members unanimously, with absolute harmony, voted to ask admission to the Congregational family.

"Mr. Bond was clearly the providential man for the transition period. The testimony was volunteered to the Council that neither by word nor deed did he or any outside persons seek to influence the church to change its connection. Their own earnestly active desire for fellowship and service prompted the transfer. Mr. Bond's acquaintance with both bodies, and particularly with the history of the local church, along with his own impartial Christian bearing made it evident that he was come to the kingdom for such a time as this.

"There were numerous surprises in connection with this notable event. The members of the Council were surprised at the evidences of important business as the entering train passed the big Mineral Point Zinc Works, employing five hundred people. Then to be met at the station by almost an auto apiece, to be whisked up and down the hills to the beautiful homes with their cordial hospitality, and to the large beautiful $30,000 home of worship capable of seating over six hundred people, and the $4,500 parsonage, added astonishment to astonishment. The audience room was decorated tastefully with autumn leaves, the attendance and music were inspiring. The reports and testimonies at the business session with the absolute harmony from the first, were exceptionally gratifying, and the whole movement seemed to be clearly of the Lord.

"Superintendent Keller was moderator and preached the sermon; Dr. Updike was scribe and gave the Right Hand of Fellowship; Brother Miner led in the Recognition Prayer; Secretary Carter gave the Charge to the People. Other parts were taken by Rev. J. Lloyd Smith and Rev. G. L. McDougal. Pastor Bond closed this memorable Council with a few warm and fitting words.

"The first Congregational Church of Mineral Point promises to be blessed and a blessing in this new relationship. Twenty-nine, all but four on confession, were received into membership at the last communion. Upon the Sabbath before the Council, one hundred and ninety-five were in attendance at the Sunday School.

"The aliveness of this church is also indicated by the active 'Alphas', the ladies' organization; the 'Coworkers', one hundred and ten of the young ladies who, among other things, are caring for the small deficit on the fine parsonage; the flourishing Brotherhood that stands back of the cost of the pipe organ to be installed next month, and of a Lecture Course held in the basement Sunday School room of the church, seating over six hundred people, and for which course six hundred season tickets were sold before the second number of the series of fine entertainments was given.

"Space fails to record others of the good things about this new Congregational partner in our common work for Christ and his Kingdom."

Thus after 1913 this congregation became known as The First Congregational Church of Mineral Point.[14]

In 1961, the members of this old congregation voted to approve the Constitution of the United Church of Christ and to affiliate with that great body. However, the members decided to retain the name, the First Congregational Church of Mineral Point, Wisconsin.

As this history is written, the Minister of the First Congregational Church is the Rev. Benjamin J. Talledge.

St. Mary's Catholic Church

The early history of the Catholics in Mineral Point has already been written in the previous pages of this chapter.

In the 1840's, 1850's and 1860's, when the German, Luxemburger, Austrian, Bohemian and Swiss emigrants arrived at Mineral Point, they and their American born children attended St. Paul's parish. Beginning in 1860 they had separate services at St. Paul's, with sermons and prayers in the German language conducted by Fr. Voissern and after him by Fr. F. X. Weinhart, both of whom came to Mineral Point on frequent occasions to conduct such services.

It gradually developed that a second Catholic church would be established at Mineral Point, and in 1870 St. Paul's congregation was divided, and St. Mary's parish was founded with the Rev. F. X. Weinhart as first pastor. During the same year the parish purchased three acres of land for $2,000 and proceeded with the erection of a frame church and a frame rectory, both of which were completed by August 1, 1870. The two buildings cost approximately $10,000. A parish school, likewise of frame construction, was completed a year later at a cost of $2,000.[15]

The cemetery of this parish is about a mile away, on the road to Madison, and was established in 1873, originally with four acres of land, later enlarged from time to time.[16]

In 1900, Rev. Nicholas Weyer was appointed pastor and under his strong leadership a large solid brick church, Roman style, was erected in 1901. The new church was 120 feet long, 46 feet wide, and 120 feet from the ground to the top of the cross.[17] A new rectory of frame construction was also erected.

In 1914 the parish installed a town clock in the tower of the church. It had four faces. Its bells struck the quarter hours as well as the hours and could be heard through most of the city.

This parish founded a large, flourishing and growing parochial grade school, which will be described in the later pages of this chapter.

As this history is written, the pastor is Father Van Handle.

Hope Lutheran Church

Lutheran services were first held in Mineral Point in 1939 with the Rev. William F. Loesch as the first pastor. A Ladies' Aid was organized and became an active factor in promoting the new congregation. Services were held in private homes and for a time in the American Legion Hall. On November 14, 1943, the group adopted the name "Hope Evangelical Lutheran Church of Mineral Point."

The congregation purchased a lot and ground breaking services were held on April 28, 1944; the cornerstone was laid on September 8, 1944; and the church edifice dedicated on April 8, 1945.

Much of the furniture for the church was received as a gift from a Lutheran congregation at Aniwa, Wisconsin. Pews were obtained from a church in Nashville, Iowa. The round stained glass window in the east wall of the church portrays Christ with a crown of thorns. The various windows were donated by the members and friends of the congregation. The Bible for the lectern was given by the Zion Lutheran Church of Bagley, Wisconsin, and the Bible for the pulpit was presented by St. Paul Lutheran Church of Burlington, Wisconsin. The hymnal for the altar was given by the Ladies' Aid Society of the American Lutheran Church of Darlington, Wisconsin.

The Hope Lutheran Church of Mineral Point has about 300 members.[18] Its pastor, in 1962, is the Rev. Harold E. Peterson.

———

In closing the historical summaries of the churches at Mineral Point, it should be mentioned that the Presbyterians organized a church in 1839, with the Rev. J. E. McQueen as minister. There were eleven original members, later increased to a hundred. In 1844 the Presbyterian congregation erected a church 44 feet by 50 feet with a bell. The cost was $3,000. This congregation was troubled with finances and beset with dissensions; the work was given up. The former church edifice became the hall of the Knights of Pythias, and later served as the gymnasium for the public high school.

The Schools

The people of Mineral Point were always strongly minded to give their children a good education. The pioneers, and later the established townspeople, pressed persistently for better and better schools.

Mineral Point has the unique distinction of having had the first non-Indian school in the area that is now

Wisconsin. That was in 1829, when the town was in Michigan Territory.[19] From then until the establishment of the public school system, there were several private schools under Protestant church leadership or under individual school masters. The history of these early Mineral Point schools is partly lost in time; still there is some information to record. The first school, opened in 1829, was established in an abandoned sod hut near the Government Spring, northeast of the present Municipal Park. Mrs. Harker was the teacher, assisted by Miss Beulah Lamb. The first year there were eight pupils, mostly from a family named Nolton. The seats consisted of wooden slabs supported by wooden pegs. The floor was made of rough wood with one side hewn flat. The children learned to write in flats of sand.

In 1830, Robert Boyer successfully solicited subscriptions for a "select school," which he opened in a good sized log cabin. Twenty pupils attended. Boyer's school lasted one or two years and closed in 1832 before the Black Hawk War.

In 1834, George Cubbage opened a school in a log cabin near what was known as Mrs. May's spring. According to the recollections of one of the pupils of this school, "The seats were so high that several years of growth were required upon the part of the little fellows before they could hope to touch their toes to the floor. From these elevated perches we were constantly dropping all sorts of articles down through the yawning cracks and receiving the benefit of lively drafts of air where our playthings went out."

In 1837, the first public school in the new Wisconsin Territory was opened at Mineral Point. It was supported by appropriations from the newly organized borough of Mineral Point and by private subscriptions when necessary.

In 1840, it was decided to erect a new public school. It was built by Joseph Turner and James Hugo at a cost of $500. It was 26 x 30 and 12 feet high, constructed of brick and stone. That winter, 1840-1841, the classes were taught by J. E. Heaton. Mineral Point was incorporated as a village in 1844, and the same year, the public schoolhouse was enlarged to provide for the rapidly increasing number of children, but the cost of the addition exhausted the available funds and in the spring of 1845 this school had to be suspended.

For a period of about five years there were only private and church schools at Mineral Point. One was taught in the stone courthouse by Dr. Losey. Another was taught by C. C. Ryerson in a log and frame structure. From 1845 to 1849 D. A. Moore conducted a school in the basement of the Methodist Church; the tuition was three dollars per term.

Mineral Point made several appropriations to the private schools; then gradually converted the private schools into public schools.

In May, 1850, shortly after Wisconsin became a State, and pursuant to improved state school laws, the public grade school was reopened with an attendance of 200 pupils. The funds raised by taxation were insufficient and pupils were asked to pay twenty-five cents per month. That caused enrollment to diminish rapidly and within the same year the public school was again closed for lack of funds.

In 1857, the Methodists erected a two story brick school which was called the Seminary. It was advertised in the Mineral Point 1859 Official Directory:[20]

MINERAL POINT SEMINARY

REV. J. NOLAN, A. M.,...................PRINCIPAL, and Teacher of Ancient Languages.

W. E. CLIFFORD, Teacher of Mathematics and Physics.

MISS A. HILDEBRAND, Preceptress, and Teacher of French and German.

CHARLES BELINSKI, Teacher of Music-Piano, Melodean and Guitar.

On all matters respecting Terms, Boarding, Books, etc., a line to the Principal will be promptly answered.

Experienced Teachers will be furnished for Schools on application to the Principal.

REFERENCES:

Hon. Parley Eaton, Mineral Point.

Hon. M. M. Cothren, Mineral Point.

Rev. M. Dinsdale, Linden.

E. Wetherbee, Esq. Shullsburg.

This institution was conducted by Rev. John Nolan until 1861, at which time it was acquired by the City of Mineral Point for the high school. The city also acquired a brick building known as the Westminister or Old School of the Presbyterian Church.

By 1861, the public school system in Mineral Point was in sound condition; a city superintendent of schools was appointed; the school system was divided into departments including a high school. There was a temporary setback in 1862 when the high school had to revert to a private status supported by tuition, but after a few months the public high school was reopened and has continued ever since.

In 1903-1904-1905 a new two story high school building was erected of cut limestone blocks. It was attractive and imposing. The dedicatory address was given by a local lawyer, E. C. Fiedler.

For the academic year 1909-1910 the Mineral Point High School issued a brochure which showed the advances made by the institution and the status it had achieved. It had, during the past year, been fully accredited by the North Central Association of Colleges, enabling graduates to enter, without examination, any college or university in the north central states. The enrollment was 168, including 54 freshmen, 42 sophomores, 40 juniors and 32 seniors. There was a faculty of seven, including the High School Principal, who was also City Superintendent of Schools. The board of education included E. C. Fiedler, president, John W. Chamley, Lawrence Gibbons, John Knight, Dr. C. G. Hubenthal, C. C. Potter, Dr. William M. Gratiot, and Wm. P. Bliss. It is interesting to note the classical education then given by the high school. There were four courses of study beginning with the comparatively easy English Course and ascending to the more difficult Classical Course: [21]

I. The English Course included four years of English reading, grammar and composition. Geography, history, algebra, geometry, physics, economics and civics.

II. The German Course was the same during the first two years, with the addition of German during the junior and senior years.

III. The Latin Course included four years of Latin, with Caesar during the second year, Cicero the third year and Virgil the fourth year.

IV. The Classical Course was much the same as the Latin Course, but added German during the third and fourth years, thus affording the gifted students one classical and one modern language.

There were no vocational courses in 1910. Manual training and domestic science were not added until September, 1913.

By 1922, the Fourth Ward Grade School was overcrowded and obsolete and it became necessary to move additional grade school classes into the high school building. A new high school building became a necessity; however the voters rejected a proposed bond issue to build one. In February, 1923, the Wisconsin State Superintendent of schools gave orders and directives which would result in terminating state aid if nothing were done. That awakened the Mineral Point voters and in 1923, by a majority of eighteen votes they approved a bond issue of $150,000. A new high school was built in 1924 and was completed for the opening of school in September, 1925. The old Fourth Ward Grade School was demolished and the grade school moved into the former high school. These arrangements were sufficient for almost a third of a century. In 1959, a major addition to the high school was completed and dedicated.[22]

As this book is written, Mineral Point is following state law and integrating the surrounding rural school districts with the city grade school and high school into Joint School District No. 1. The plan will strengthen the public school system. The grade school presents no problem, although the projected development of the high school may leave it somewhat smaller than desired. When completely organized the integrated school district will have an equalized assessed value for tax purposes of some $18,500,000. The school district is governed by a board of seven of whom two are elected from the rural areas. There are thirty-four teachers on the faculty in the public school system and at least two of them have Master's Degrees.

In September, 1960, the enrollment in the city and rural grade schools totaled 426. In the high school there were 69 freshmen, 56 sophomores, 69 juniors and 46 seniors, making a total of 240.

In September 1961, the enrollment in the city and rural grade schools totaled 449. In the high school there were 72 freshmen, 72 sophomores, 52 juniors, and 64 seniors, making a total of 260.

In April 1962, there were already 95 registered for the freshman class to enter in September; and the projections indicated that the enrollment of the Mineral Point High School would soon exceed 300.

Catholic Schools

As early as 1846 or 1847 in territorial times before Wisconsin became a state, Fr. Victor Jouanneault, a French priest, and at that time pastor of St. Paul's parish, erected a small red brick building in which he opened a Catholic grade school and served as its first teacher. The second teacher was Miss Mary Torphy and the next was John Cummins. The records of this school are meager.

On October 10, 1868, the Dominican motherhouse at Sinsinawa Mound sent Sister Mary Josephine Cahill and Sister Alphonsa Seely to St. Paul's parish to establish a parochial school. For the next fifteen years the Dominicans from Sinsinawa conducted a Catholic grade school, but the enrollment was small and in July, 1883, these sisters withdrew and this school was closed. However, there were two parochial grade schools that were open at Mineral Point during the twelve years from 1871 to 1883.[23]

After St. Mary's parish was founded in 1870, plans were laid immediately for the erection of a parochial school building. It was completed by September, 1871, at a cost of $2,000. It was located on what is now the front playground. It was equipped with two school rooms, one on the first floor and another on the second. There was also a small chapel with a few pews on the first floor. This school was opened on October 19, 1871, with two teaching nuns and an enrollment of seventy-five pupils. The teachers at this school were also Dominicans, but from St. Catherine's motherhouse at Racine, Wisconsin. Two years later in 1873, the enrollment had grown and a third teaching sister was added. From 1874 to 1906 there were only two teaching sisters at this school, but commencing in 1906 a third teacher was added permanently. There were then only seven grades in the school. The first school house lasted one generation; then needed replacement. In

1904 the old frame structure was replaced with the present large red brick school building. The east one-third of the brick structure was constructed as the convent residence for the teaching nuns and was thus occupied continuously from 1904 during the ensuing forty-seven years.

In September, 1917, the school added the eighth grade; thereafter it became possible for the graduates of St. Mary's parochial school to go directly into a high school, public or private.

In 1935 through the efforts of Bishop McGavick, the children whose families were members of St. Paul's parish began to attend St. Mary's School, and the enrollment was increased by forty-eight new pupils. This sharp increase in enrollment necessitated the addition of a fourth teacher.

In 1951, the enrollment increased again; more classrooms were needed; the nuns moved out of the school building into a nearby residence and thereby made space available for additional school rooms.

In September, 1959, a fifth teacher was added on account of the further increase in enrollment caused by the closing of rural one-room schools. During the term which ended in June, 1961, this school was staffed by five teachers, three nuns and two lay teachers. The school then became faced with the necessity to expand once again on account of the closing of more rural schools and the growing size of families. The increasing enrollment is reflected in the following table: [24]

School Year	*Number of Pupils*
1871-1872	75
1901-1902	101
1935-1936 (Children from St. Paul's Parish added)	133
1959-1960 (Rural schools closing)	200
1960-1961	212
1961-1962	233

During the summer of 1961, the parochial school faced many problems: a sharply increasing enrollment; a building that was 57 years old and in need of complete renovation; a need to raise almost $150,000; and the serious shortage of teaching nuns. (Although the absolute number of women in religious orders has gradually increased in the United States, the population has increased more rapidly and the demand for teaching nuns has increased at an even greater rate. Thus in 1950 there were 82,000 teaching sisters and 13,000 lay teachers or a ratio of 6 to 1. In 1960 there were 98,000 teaching sisters to 45,000 lay teachers or a ratio of about 2 to 1.)

All the foregoing problems of The Catholic School at Mineral Point were solved under the leadership of Bishop William P. O'Conner of Madison and the two local Pastors, Fr. Mueller and Fr. Grasso. The classrooms in the old red brick building and the former living quarters of the nuns were torn out and eight modern classrooms were constructed, together with library and music rooms. In addition the lighting, heating and plumbing facilities were completely modernized. Work was also commenced on the construction of a 42x92 foot addition on the west side of the brick building. The new wing was designed to serve many purposes: a gymnasium, a meeting hall, a school lunch area to serve as many as 350 children or adults at one sitting. The Dominicans of Racine sent another teaching nun, raising their staff to four. With the two lay teachers, there was a total staff of six teachers, aside from the other employees of the school. The financial problem was handled by the cooperative efforts of the two parishes, which arranged to divide the cost and pay the debt over a period of several years.

NOTES

Churches:

[1] Wisconsin Historical Collections, Vol. XV, p. 291.

[2] History of Iowa County, Wisconsin, (Chicago, 1881), p. 714.

[3] Ibid., p. 600.

[4] Ibid., p. 716.

[5] Ibid.

[6] Mazzuchelli, O. P., Rev. Samuel, Memoirs (Chicago: W. F. Hall Printing Co., 1915), p. 157.

[7] The Iowa County Democrat and Mineral Point Tribune, Centennial Edition, Section 4, p. 5.

[8] Inama, Letters, p. 66.

[9] Ibid., p. 85.

[10] Catholic Almanac, 1846. In the Salzmann Library, St. Francis Major Seminary, Milwaukee.

[11] The Iowa County Democrat and Mineral Point Tribune, Centennial Edition, Section 4, p. 5.

[12] Ibid., p. 4.

[13] Wisconsin Territorial Papers, County Series, Iowa County, (Madison, Wisconsin. Wisconsin State Historical Society, 1942.) Vol. II, p. 103.

[14] Letter, October, 1961, from First Congregational Church to the author.

[15] History of Iowa County, supra, p. 723.

[16] Ibid.

[17] The Iowa County Democrat and Mineral Point Tribune, Centennial Edition, Section 4, p. 4.

[18] Ibid.

Schools:

[19] Stearns, J. W., *Columbian History of Education in Wisconsin*, pp. 586, 587.

[20] Official Directory, 1859. Compiled by J. S. Allen.

[21] Mineral Point High School 1910 Greetings.

[22] *Democrat Tribune*, September 17, 1959. Dedication Section.

[23] O'Connor, *Five Decades*, (1954) The Sinsinawa Press, p. 161.

[24] Letter, March, 1960, from the Archivist of Dominican Mother House at Racine to George Fiedler.

XVII.

The Population of Mineral Point

National Origins

THERE HAS always been much loose talk in Mineral Point about the size of its population. There may be some doubt about the exact figures in 1830 and 1840. However, after that the decennial census figures give precise answers: [1]

Year	Population of Mineral Point
1830 (estimated)	500
1840 (estimated)	1500
1850	2110
1860	2389
1870	3275
1880	2915
1890	2694
1900	2991
1910	2925
1920	2569
1930	2274
1940	2275
1950	2284
1960	2384

It is interesting to note that in 1830 Milwaukee had an estimated population of between 1 and 10. In 1840, Milwaukee's population was 1,712.

The most striking analysis is that in 1860 the population of the entire United States was 31,443,321, which by 1960 had multiplied almost six times to 180,000,000. If Mineral Point had merely kept pace, its 1860 population of 2,389 would by 1960 have multiplied by six and have grown to almost 14,000. But the fact is that during the course of a century, Mineral Point's population has declined. The reasons for the decline have been outlined in this book.

As to the population of Iowa County, the figures show the following:

Year	Population Iowa County
1840	3,978
1850	9,525
1870	24,544
1900	23,114
1950	19,610
1960	19,489

The foregoing table shows that the population of the farming area surrounding Mineral Point has been declining for several decades. That trend was nation wide. In 1910 one out of every three persons in the United States lived on a farm. In 1960 less than one in eight lived on a farm.

As to the national origins of the people of Mineral Point, the previous pages of this book have shown that the first non-French, in fact the first considerable Anglo-Saxon settlement in what is now Wisconsin, was at Mineral Point. Those first settlers were of English extraction and the next were the Cornish immigrants. In the later years the town took on added ethnic elements, the Irish, the Germans, the Italians and the others. Now, in 1961, it is impossible to give precise answers, because there have been too many boundary changes in the mother countries of the old world, too many cross marriages among the nationalities in the new world, and too many changes of names. At the same time it is possible to establish and outline the main facts, figures and percentages.

At the time of discovery, this region was inhabited by the Indians, very few in numbers. They were the only Americans; all who came later were immigrants. The original Thirteen Colonies on the Atlantic were overwhelmingly of English descent, with a large colony of Germans in Pennsylvania, and with scattered groups of other nationalities. In 1760, the population of the Thirteen Colonies was approximately 1,600,000, about one-fourth of whom were negro slaves. In the Great Lakes area, there were a few widely separated French settlements, historically important but numerically containing only a handful of French. In 1820 the population of the United States was 9,638,453; in 1830 was 12,860,020.

After the days of the colonial settlements, and after the American Revolution, the great mother countries of Europe sent to America a flood of peoples who came year after year and decade after decade. One of the greatest movements of populations in all history. Statistics on immigration into the United States began to be recorded in 1820. Since 1820, some 40,000,000 immigrants entered the United States. Of those it is estimated that 35,000,000 came to stay.

In the previous pages of this book, it was mentioned that the two cabins found in Mineral Point in

1827 were occupied, one by a minister named Elder William Roberts (presumably of English background) and the other "was owned by a German by the name of Christopher Law." In the "History of Iowa County," published in 1881, it is said: "The inhabitants embrace several nationalities, among which the English and Germans predominate." [2] It is clear that by English, the author meant to include the Cornish and the Welsh.

In order to summarize the basic facts as to immigration, national descent, population and ethnic elements in the United States and so in Mineral Point, the following table is instructive:

Principal sources of immigration from five leading countries to the United States and numbers during 124 years beginning 1820 and ending June 30, 1943:

Mother Country	Population in 1955	Peak Year of Immigration	Total 124 Yrs.	Per Cent of Total
Germany	71,500,000	1882	6,028,377	15.96
Italy	48,000,000	1907	4,719,825	12.49
Ireland	2,900,000	1851	4,592,595	12.16
Great Britain	51,200,000	1888	4,264,728	11.29
Austria Hungary	51,400,000 (in 1910)	1907	4,144,366	10.97
All others				37.13
				100.00%

More than a score of other countries comprise all the others and make up the remainder.

By applying the foregoing national figures to Mineral Point, and by adjusting those figures to well-known local history the ethnic elements in and around Mineral Point from first to last are English (including the Cornish and Welsh), next German (including

the Luxemburgers), next Irish, next Italian. And all
the others have contributed their part to the American amalgam as well.

NOTES

[1] Letter, July 16, 1959, from Howard G. Brunsman, Chief, Population Division, Bureau of Census to George Fiedler.

[2] *History of Iowa County, Wisconsin* (Chicago, 1881), p. 651.

XVIII.

The Town in the Hills

MINERAL POINT is an old town, lying in the most ancient hills and valleys and rocks in the middlewest. If any one wants to know what a region looked like before the last Ice Age, let him journey to Mineral Point, Wisconsin.

After the prehistoric mound builders or Indians, the recorded history of this area may be summarized by the following table:

France	1634 to 1763
England	1763 to 1794
The United States, Virginia and Ohio	1794 to 1800
Indiana Territory	1800 to 1809
Illinois Territory	1809 to 1818
Michigan Territory	1818 to 1836
Wisconsin Territory	1836 to 1848
State of Wisconsin	1848

When first settled in 1827, this rugged place contained picturesque primeval hills and valleys, covered with tall grasses, wild flowers and a few scattered groves. A beautiful region. Beginning with the discovery of lead in 1828, it was converted into a raw, grimy mining camp, pockmarked everywhere with the diggings of prospectors and miners. There were also mine shafts with piles of rocks and dirt on all sides. All the trees for miles around were cut down for firewood to operate the lead smelters. After the lead mines began to be exhausted in 1847 and later, the miners gradually turned to farming, particularly wheat farming, and the tortured terrain partially recovered as nature did its work.

After the development of zinc, the mining companies opened very deep mines and the surface of the earth was again pulled apart and piles of rocks and tailings grew to enormous artificial mounds. The zinc oxide furnace and sulphuric acid plant made Mineral Point into a prosperous place but also a grim town with industrial wastes spoiling the streams, and noxious fumes fouling the air.

Next in history came the ten or twelve year depression, with panic, hard times, a declining population, a discouraged people, a town that grew more shabby day by day. Then again the hard times ended and Mineral Point became prosperous.

The miners were totally unconcerned about the appearance of their town; that tendency has continued, generation after generation. The town continues to reveal the effects of the mining days, of the vast ruins of the zinc works and its spoil area. Somewhat recently the people have awakened to the natural charm of their city and have made progress in changing the appearance of the place from an old mining and smelting town to a village with irregular and picturesque streets and alleys and with well-kept homes, lawns and gardens.

The historic sites and buildings have recently been marked with attractive signs. An appropriate tour has been laid out by Robert M. Neal of Pendarvis House. The cover of the guide folder was designed by Mrs. Katherine Ely Ingraham. The following is a summary of the thirty-nine sites which have been marked as places of interest:

Historic Site Number

1. Methodist Church. The third structure of this faith in the community. It was built of white sandstone, was dedicated in 1871.

2. Trinity Episcopal Church, a red brick building of Gothic design. It was consecrated by Bishop Jackson Kemper in August, 1855. Trinity Parish is the second oldest parish in the Wisconsin Episcopalian Diocese. Gov. Henry Dodge, Moses M. Strong and Gen. William R. Smith were early members.

3. Thomas Priestley house, a brick structure of Pennsylvania Dutch design.

4. Alexander Wilson house, a two-story red brick building. Wilson was a distinguished lawyer. He served two terms as Attorney General of Wisconsin.

5. Henry Plowman house, a two-story limestone residence built in 1855. Plowman was co-founder of the *Miner's Free Press.*

6. William A. Jones house, a contemporary red brick residence. Jones, of Welsh descent, came to this area in 1851. He served as Superintendent of the Iowa County schools and was an original stockholder in the Mineral Point Zinc Company. In 1897 President McKinley appointed him U. S. Commissioner of Indian Affairs, a post he filled for eight years.

7. St. Paul's Catholic Church. At the rear is a one-story
& limestone building erected in 1842 which served the
8. parish as a church and school.

9. Moses M. Strong house. Strong came to Mineral Point in 1836 and opened a law and land agency office. He assisted in the survey of the present city of Madison, which was laid out in 1837. In 1838 he was appointed

U. S. District Attorney for the Territory of Wisconsin. In 1846 he was elected delegate to the Constitutional Convention. He was actively engaged in promoting railroad construction throughout the state. In the latter part of his life he served as vice president of the State Historical Society and president of the State Bar Association. His "History of Wisconsin" is one of the authoritative books on the early Territory and State.

10. Montgomery M. Cothren house, erected in 1855. Cothren served as a delegate to the Territorial Legislature of 1847-48. He became a member of the State Senate and in 1852 was elected Judge of the Fifth Judicial Circuit, an office he held for 12 years.

11. William Lanyon house, a large red-brick residence with a square tower. Built in 1857. Lanyon established an iron foundry which, during the course of its operation, made many of the iron galleries, fences and decorative iron products seen in this community. He also perfected and patented a machine for crushing ore.

12. The old non-sectarian Mineral Point cemetery. In this cemetery the early settlers were buried, including John and Matilda Hood, the first permanent white settlers at Mineral Point.

13. Congregational Church. A large stucco-covered building constructed in 1892. On this site stood the old stone Primitive Methodist Church, erected in 1848.

14. Jerusalem Park, so named after a spring which furnished early settlers with drinking water and to which Elder Roberts came, usually singing the old hymn "Jerusalem, My Happy Home."

15. Cyrus Woodman house, a remodelled three-story residence with balconies extending across the front. Woodman came to Mineral Point in 1844 and formed a partnership with C. C. Washburn in law and banking.

16. The Washburn and Woodman Bank, a two-story remodelled red brick building established in 1852. Washburn moved to LaCrosse in 1859, served in the Civil War, was elected Congressman and in 1871 became Governor of Wisconsin. Defeated for a second term, he

retired to business life and was one of the founders of the Washburn and Crosby Flour Milling Company of Minnesota, now known as General Mills.

17. Dr. Harmon Van Duesen house. Dr. Van Duesen began his practice in Mineral Point in 1848 and became a leading physician of the community. In 1868 and 1872 he was president of the Wisconsin Medical Society.

18. Site of the United States Land Office, established in 1834 for the sale of public lands in the newly organized Wisconsin Land District. It was to this office that every miner, farmer, merchant and smelter came to enter his land claims.

19. Site of Presbyterian Church. The frame structure once occupying this site was dedicated in 1844, the congregation having been organized under leadership of the Rev. James E. Quaw, a noted pioneer preacher.

20. United States Hotel, a three-story limestone structure built about 1855. This hostelry served the community for many years. Ulysses S. Grant stayed here while working on a geological survey of the region.

21. On the site of the present municipal building was the old Iowa County Courthouse and log jail. In 1835, a two-story log building was erected on this public square. In 1842 the old building was sold at auction. In 1843 a new Courthouse built of stone was completed.

22. Oddfellow's Hall. A two-story, yellow frame building built in 1839. This building erected by Iowa Lodge No. 1, is the first Oddfellow's building West of the Alleghenies.

23. Depot of the Mineral Point railroad, constructed of limestone. It was built in 1857 when the railroad came to the city.

24. Walker Hotel. This stone building was constructed at three different periods. The right section first; then the far left. In the 1860's, the two buildings were joined by a third section. This hotel served the area over a period of many years.

25. Legend tells us that an early prospector traveling on horseback first discovered the "mineral" on this "point"

of land. To the left on this ridge were the original lead mining diggins.

26. Site of legal hanging in the territory of Wisconsin carried out on November 1, 1842. About 5,000 persons sat on the hillsides to watch the execution.

27. Site of Fort Jackson, built in 1832 during the Blackhawk War. The stockade consisted of a large, square enclosure built of logs set in the ground. There were two entrances, one at this corner and another at the Northwest, each with a block house and sentry box. In the center of the enclosure stood several cabins, refuges for miners and their families. During the Blackhawk War, Fort Jackson was an important center for the distribution of military supplies to other Forts in this area.

28. Site of the Mansion House, the most famous tavern in the mining area. To it came people from all walks of life; from the crude prospector to the educated jurist. The building consisted of a series of log cabins of various sizes connected by passageways.

29. Site of Mark Terrill's Inn, also known in the early days as The Stagg Inn, where according to one old settler: "Hell and damnation broke loose every Saturday and Sunday night."

30. Site of the First Methodist Episcopal Church, constructed in 1834. The 24 x 30 foot building was constructed entirely of logs; the floor and the seats were of split logs. This was the first Protestant Church erected in Wisconsin.

31. Entrance to the Soldiers' Memorial Park, a recreational area with picnic facilities.

32. Pendarvis House, a nationally known restoration of early Cornish houses. This group of three houses was constructed in the early 1830's. The rock houses of this group are typical of the cottages in Cornwall, England.

33. Rock buildings of the old Mineral Springs Brewery.

34. Site of John Clowney's shop. Clowney came to Mineral Point in 1839 and built the first carpenter and tool shop in this region, supplying many of the early settlers with cabinet work.

35. Henry Rodolf House. A limestone structure with three dormer windows. This house was constructed in the 1840's and later was the home of Judge Samuel Crawford, an Associate Justice of the Wisconsin Supreme Court.

36. Ansley House, a two-story frame building with four tall, fluted columns. The Ansley family came from the South, which accounts for this architectural style of a southern plantation home.

37. St. Mary's Catholic Church and school. The present building replaces an early frame structure.

38. Mineral Point Historical Society Museum which contains displays of local and state interest. A particularly noteworthy mineral collection, one of the finest in the Middle West, is housed in this Museum.

39. John Terry home. The original one-story frame building with a veranda the full length of the front has been remodelled and enlarged. Terry came to the lead region in 1829 as a merchant and smelter, served in the Blackhawk War as Captain under Henry Dodge, and was a member of the Territorial Legislature.

This book has outlined the history of this town, but no one should think of Mineral Point as merely a historical monument. It has had many lives, it is now again increasing in population, its future as a small city is secure. Mineral Point is one of the few relics of the early days, a place where one can, if so minded, live in houses and enjoy surroundings established before Wisconsin became a state. Of approximately seventy-six buildings pictured in "Historic Wisconsin Architecture" ten are in Mineral Point:

Ingraham House, the 1830's.

Pendarvis House, *circa* 1835.

Polperro House, *circa* 1835.

Odd Fellows Hall, built 1838.

Trinity Episcopal Church, completed 1846.
Mineral Point Brewery, built 1850.
213 Clowney Street, *circa* 1850.
Old Railroad Station, built 1857.
138 High Street, *circa* 1860.
Moses M. Strong House, 1868.

One author, David Van Tassel, wrote a dissertation entitled "Democracy, Fontier and Mineral Point; A Study of the Influence of the Frontier on a Wisconsin Mining Town." Van Tassel found that in territorial times the social structure of the population of Mineral Point was a typical mixture of rough mining men and high territorial officials, some of whom had an excellent education. Van Tassel also stated that in the later middle years the population became class conscious, based on financial and educational differences, and that the status symbols of the upper classes were Trinity Episcopal Church, the Freemasons, and The Lyceum.

Mineral Point has had several historians. William R. Smith wrote his *History of Wisconsin* at Mineral Point; he dedicated his work to the people of the State of Wisconsin on July 4, 1854. The *History of Iowa County, Wisconsin,* containing the early history of Mineral Point, was published in 1881. Moses M. Strong wrote his *History of the Territory of Wisconsin* in his house at Mineral Point; he published his book in 1885. *The Mineral Point History and Guide* was written by a group of writers as a work project during the depression of the 1930's but was never printed or published. *Frontiersman of Fortune: Moses M. Strong of Mineral Point* by Kenneth M. Duckett was published by the State Historical Society of Wisconsin in 1955. *Westernized Yankee. The Story of Cyrus Woodman* by Larry Gara was published by the State Historical Society of Wisconsin in 1956. August Derleth published his historical novel *The Hills Stand Watch* in 1959. This history of Mineral Point was completed in 1962.

The End

Bibliography

Books

Catholic Almanac 1846 (F. Lucas, Jr., Baltimore) In the Salzmann Library at St. Francis Major Seminary, Milwaukee.

History and Guide to Mineral Point (W. P. A. Federal Writers' Project, State Historical Society of Wisconsin, Madison).

History of Iowa County, Wisconsin, Western Historical Company, (Chicago, 1881).

Wisconsin, a Guide to the Badger State (Washington: Works Progress Administration, 1941).

AMBERG, JOHN ADAMS, *Family Record*, translated from the German by William A. Amberg; revised and edited by Gilbert A. Amberg. (Chicago: Privately published, 1934).

DERLETH, AUGUST, *The Wisconsin* (New York: Farrar and Rinehart, 1942).

———. *The Hills Stand Watch* (New York: Duell, Sloan and Pearce, 1960).

DUCKETT, KENNETH W., *Frontiersman of Fortune: Moses M. Strong of Mineral Point* (Madison: State Historical Society of Wisconsin, 1955).

FEATHERSTONHAUGH, G. W., *A Canoe Voyage Up The Minnay Sotor* (London, 1847, Richard Bentley).

FIEDLER, GEORGE, *Fiedler Family*, 1648 - 1946 (Winnetka: Privately published, 1946).

GARRY, LARRY, *Westernized Yankee. The Story of Cyrus Woodman* (Madison, State Historical Society of Wisconsin, 1956).

HAGEN, WILLIAM THOMAS, *Black Hawk's Route Through Wisconsin* (Madison: State Historical Society of Wisconsin, 1949).

HOBBS, MERVILLE K., *John and Sarah Bradbury Coons and Their Descendants* (Chicago: Privately published, 1939).

HOLMES, FRED L., *Letters of the Reverend Adelbert Inama,* translated from the German (Evansville: State Historical Society of Wisconsin).

HUNT, ROBERT S., *Law and Locomotives* (Madison: State Historical Society of Wisconsin, 1958).

JOHNSON, REV. PETER LEO, *Crosier on The Frontier* (Madison: State Historical Society of Wisconsin, 1959).

KELLOGG, LOUISE P., *The French Regime in Wisconsin and The Northwest* (State Historical Society of Wisconsin, Madison, 1925).

MAZZUCHELLI, SAMUEL, *Memoirs of Father Mazzuchelli, O.P.,* translated from the Italian (Chicago, 1915).

"MORLEIGH," *A Merry Briton in Pioneer Wisconsin* (London, 1842. The State Historical Society of Wisconsin, 1950).

O'CONNOR, SISTER PASCHALA, O.P., *Five Decades* (The Sinsinawa Press, Sinsinawa, Wisconsin, 1954).

Peoples of Wisconsin (Madison: State Historical Society of Wisconsin, 1955).

RANEY, WILLIAM FRANCIS, *Wisconsin, A Story of Progress* (New York, 1940, Prentice-Hall, Inc.).

REED, PARKER McCOBB, *The Bench and Bar of Wisconsin,* (Milwaukee, 1882).

SCHAFER, JOSEPH, *The Wisconsin Lead Region* (Madison: State Historical Society of Wisconsin, 1942).

SMITH, ALICE E., *James Duane Doty* (Madison: State Historical Society of Wisconsin, 1954).

SMITH, WILLIAM R., *Incidents of a Journey from Pennsylvania to Wisconsin Territory in 1837.*

SMITH, WILLIAM R. OF MINERAL POINT, *History of Wisconsin* (Madison, 1854).

STEARNS, J. W., *Columbian History of Education in Wisconsin* (Milwaukee: 1893, Evening Wisconsin Company).

STRONG, MOSES M., *History of the Wisconsin Territory* (Madison: Democrat Printing Co., 1885).

SWANTON, JOHN R., *The Indian Tribes of North America* (Washington: United States Government Printing Office, 1953).

THWAITS, REUBEN GOLD, *The Story of Wisconsin* (Boston: Lothrop Publishing Company, 1891).

TUTTLE, CHARLES R., *Illustrated History of Wisconsin* (Madison, B. B. Russell & Co., 1875).

USHER, ELLIS BAKER, *Wisconsin* Vol. I (New York: The Lewis Publishing Company, 1914).

VAN TASSEL, DAVID, *"Democracy, Frontier and Mineral Point: A Study of the Influence of the Frontier on a Wisconsin Mining Town."* 1957 M. S. Thesis. In Library of the University of Wisconsin.

Wisconsin Blue Book, 1911.

Wisconsin Historical Collections, 20 volumes.

Wisconsin Territorial Papers, County Series, Iowa County (Madison, Wisconsin. Wisconsin State Historical Society, 1942. Vols. I and II).

WRIGHT, G. FREDERICK, *Man and the Glacial Period* (New York: D. Appleton and Company, 1898).

Magazines

Wisconsin Magazine of History, Vol. 29, No. 2 (June, 1946).

National Geographic Magazine, Vol. III, No. 2 (February, 1947).

Holiday, Vol. 23, No. 6 (June, 1958).

America, Vol. CII, No. 25 (March 26, 1960) "Can We Keep On Paying for Catholic Schools?"

Newspapers and Pamphlets

Mineral Point, The Wisconsin *Tribune*, September 3, 1847. (First Edition).

Mineral Point Tribune, 1849 - 1932.

Mineral Point, *The Iowa County Democrat* and *The Mineral Point Tribune*, October 9, 1947, Centennial Edition.

Directory of the City of Mineral Point for the Year 1959. Compiled by J. S. Allen. In the Library of The Chicago Historical Society, Chicago, Illinois.

Mineral Point High School 1910 Greetings. In the Library of the State Historical Society of Wisconsin.

Address of Hon. M. M. Strong, Delivered at Mineral Point, July 4th, 1861. In the Free Public Library of Mineral Point.

Reported Decisions of the Courts

United States vs. *Gear*, 3 How. Rep. 120.

Iowa County vs. *Green County*, (1845) Pinney's Reports 518.

State ex rel Cothren vs. *Joseph Lean* (1859) 9 Wis. 279.

Christopher L. Williams as receiver of the First National Bank of Mineral Point vs. *John P. Cobb* (1914) 2nd Cir., 219 Fed. 663, Aff'd. (1916) 242 U. S. 307; 61 L. Ed. 325.

Christopher L. Williams as receiver of the First National Bank of Mineral Point vs. *Calvert Spensley, James Brewer, John L. Gray, William P. Gundry, et al.* (1917) 7th Cir., 251 Fed. 58.